European Competence Standards for the Academic Training of Career Practitioners

European Competence Standards for the Academic Training of Career Practitioners

NICE Handbook Volume II

Edited by

Christiane Schiersmann, Sif Einarsdóttir, Johannes Katsarov, Jukka Lerkkanen, Rachel Mulvey, Jacques Pouyaud, Kestutis Pukelis, and Peter Weber

Barbara Budrich Publishers
Opladen • Berlin • Toronto 2016

All rights reserved. No part of this publication may be reproduced, stored in or introduced into a retrieval system, or transmitted, in any form, or by any means (electronic, mechanical, photocopying, recording or otherwise) without the prior written permission of Barbara Budrich Publishers. Any person who does any unauthorized act in relation to this publication may be liable to criminal prosecution and civil claims for damages. You must not circulate this book in any other binding or cover and you must impose this same condition on any acquirer.

Items marked as "Open Educational Resources" are exempt from this provision: Provided their source is acknowledged, and their content isn't manipulated, they may be copied and distributed freely.

The NICE Handbook is a publication of the Network for Innovation in Career Guidance and Counselling in Europe (NICE), an academic network of 46 higher education institutions in 30 European countries, which is funded with financial support from the European Commission under the Lifelong Learning Programme from 2009-2015. The European Commission's support for the production of this publication does not constitute an endorsement of the contents which reflects the views only of the authors, and the Commission cannot be held responsible for any use which may be made of the information contained therein.

A CIP catalogue record for this book is available from
Die Deutsche Bibliothek (The German Library)

© 2016 by Barbara Budrich Publishers, Opladen, Berlin & Toronto
Stauffenbergstr. 7. D-51379 Leverkusen Opladen, Germany
86 Delma Drive. Toronto, ON M8W 4P6 Canada
www.barbara-budrich.net

    ISBN   978-3-8474-0504-7 (Paperback)
    eISBN 978-3-8474-0925-5 (eBook)

Das Werk einschließlich aller seiner Teile ist urheberrechtlich geschützt. Jede Verwertung außerhalb der engen Grenzen des Urheberrechtsgesetzes ist ohne Zustimmung des Verlages unzulässig und strafbar. Das gilt insbesondere für Vervielfältigungen, Übersetzungen, Mikroverfilmungen und die Einspeicherung und Verarbeitung in elektronischen Systemen.

Die Deutsche Bibliothek – CIP-Einheitsaufnahme
Ein Titeldatensatz für die Publikation ist bei Der Deutschen Bibliothek erhältlich.

Layout and graphic design: Sonya Stefanova Katsarova, Konstanz, Germany
Typographical editing: Judith Henning, Hamburg, Germany
Editing: Alison Romer, Lancaster, UK
Printed in Europe on acid-free paper by Elanders GmbH, Waiblingen, Germany

Content

Editorial	9
Memorandum on Academic Training and Research in Career Guidance and Counselling	11
1. Introduction	15
1.1 Purpose of the Handbook	17
1.2 Structure	20
2. Goals and Design of the European Competence Standards	23
2.1 Background	25
2.2 Goals	26
2.3 Challenges	28
2.4 Design of the Competence Standards	32
3. Three Types of Career Practitioners	35
3.1 The NICE Professional Roles Revisited	37
3.2 The NICE Types of Career Practitioners	40
3.3 Task Profiles	44
3.3.1 Task Profile of Career Advisors	45
3.3.2 Task Profile of Career Professionals	46
3.3.3 Task Profiles of Career Specialists	46

4. European Competence Standards — 49

4.1 Competence Definition — 51

4.2 Formulation of Competence Standards — 52

4.3 The European Competence Standards — 54

4.4 Using the ECS for Curriculum Development — 54

4.4.1 Examples — 55

4.4.2 Working with the NICE Curriculum Framework — 60

5. Recommended Qualification Levels — 63

5.1 Recommended Qualification Levels — 65

5.2 Elaboration of Recommended Qualification Levels — 66

5.2.1 Career Advisors — 67

5.2.2 Career Professionals — 71

5.2.3 Career Specialists — 74

6. Quality Assurance and Enhancement: Policy and Practice — 79

6.1 Policy Drivers — 81

6.2 How NICE supports Quality Assurance and Enhancement — 84

7. Peer Learning for the Quality Enhancement of Degree Programmes — 89

7.1 Peer Learning in the Context of Academic Training — 91

7.1.1 Peer Learning as a Method for Quality Enhancement — 91

7.1.2 Five Principles for Quality Enhancement through Peer Learning — 92

7.2 Peer Learning in Practice: Three Case Studies — 94

7.2.1 Moderation of Peer Learning Activities — 94

7.2.2 Description of Three Peer-Learning Activities — 96

7.3 Guidelines for Peer Learning — 98

7.4 Opportunities and Challenges of Peer Learning — 103

ACKNOWLEDGEMENTS	**107**

APPENDIX	**111**
Appendix 1: The Bergen Communiqué (Bergen 2005)	113
Appendix 2: Resources to Support Quality Assurance	115

REFERENCES	**117**

THE NICE GLOSSARY	**125**

MAP OF PARTNERS	**134**

LIST OF PARTNERS	**135**

Editorial

Dear Readers,

This handbook for the academic training of career practitioners is a joint production of the "Network for Innovation in Career Guidance and Counselling in Europe" (NICE), which spans across almost all European countries. In this volume, we present common European Competence Standards for the Academic Training of Career Practitioners, competence standards which we have worked out collaboratively over the past 3 years.

"We" refers to the partners of the project NICE 2, which has been funded substantially by the European Commission from 2012-2015. You will find an overview of the 46 project partners from 30 countries at the end of this publication. Most of us offer degree programmes in career guidance and counselling (CGC), are currently setting up such programmes, or conduct research related to this practice. From 2009-2012, the majority of us have already worked together in the project NICE 1, ending with the publication of the first volume of the NICE Handbook. We feel very honoured that the work of NICE is supported by a large number of actors, including representatives of many other degree programmes in Europe, who have not been formal partners of the project leading to this publication.

As a consortium of specialists in the academic training of career practitioners and CGC-related research, our mission is to promote professionalism and excellence in career guidance and counselling. The NICE Memorandum (on the following two pages) formulates our vision for the development of academic training and research in the area of career guidance and counselling in Europe. There, we express three central challenges for the professionalization of career guidance and counselling, which we want to tackle in the near future:

1. The needs for high quality, competence-based academic training of career practitioners and for common European competence standards;

2. The needs for interdisciplinary research on career guidance and counselling, the training of excellent researchers and setting up an international research community;

3. The needs for bridging the gaps between research, theory, practice and policy, and for enhancing the existing cooperation between the different actors in the field.

In this handbook, we present some of the central outcomes of the collaboration in NICE. To the largest extent, we have concentrated on the first challenge articulated in the NICE Memorandum over the past six years: academic training. We are proud to finalise this project by having reached a consensus about the training needs for career practitioners in Europe, more precisely the first edition of European Competence Standards, which we present in this publication. Additionally, we are happy that through the six international conferences, numerous workshops and hundreds of virtual meetings, we have managed to intensify our international relations in Europe. In doing so, we have not only set up an academic network, which we can draw upon in the future. In line with the third point of the NICE Memorandum, we have also been able to involve practitioners and policy makers from all over Europe in our work and to build ties with them, through which we can also improve cooperation in the future.

We would like to thank the European Commission for its support of the project, which led to this publication. A serious exchange about academic training in career guidance and counselling can almost only take place at a transnational level – at least in Europe. The achievements of our network would hardly have been possible without the financial funding through the Lifelong Learning Programme. In addition to the fruitful exchange and joint development, NICE has also enriched all of us with a deeper understanding of different cultures. Moreover, it has let us share the positive experience of being part of a European community.

Furthermore, we would like to express our gratitude to all people and organisations, who have contributed to the discussion on which competences are needed in the field of career guidance and counselling. On the one hand, we would like to thank all the actors, who have developed relevant quality and competence frameworks in the past: You have set the field for the endeavour of establishing competence standards in Europe. On the other hand, we would like to thank the participants of the European Summit on Developing the Career Workforce of the Future in Canterbury (2014) and the people who participated in our public consultation on the European Competence Standards. You have helped us refine our concepts and ensure that the first edition of the competence standards has also reflected perspectives, which weren't present in the draft of the framework.

Finally, as the editors of this handbook, we would like to thank our colleagues from NICE very much for their high level of trust, hoping that we have lived up to this responsibility. It has been a great pleasure for us to develop the concepts presented in this handbook together with such a lively and dedicated community, and we hope that this handbook will help to disseminate our joint products and put them into practice.

Johannes Katsarov, Sif Einarsdóttir, Jukka Lerkkanen, Rachel Mulvey, Jacques Pouyaud, Kestutis Pukelis, Christiane Schiersmann and Peter Weber (The Editing Team)

Heidelberg, 30th of September 2015

Memorandum on Academic Training and Research in Career Guidance and Counselling

Bratislava, the 30th of May 2015[1]

NICE calls upon all scholars and representatives of higher education institutions, all practitioners, associations and policy makers working in the field of career guidance and counselling to contribute actively to three fields of action for the future development of career guidance and counselling in Europe.

High Quality Competence-based Academic Training

The practice of career guidance and counselling requires substantial training, combining theory, practice and research. To attract motivated students to train as career practitioners, requirements need to be matched to what we want to offer in terms of high quality academic training. In turn, this opens up good career prospects for practitioners. Furthermore, career practitioners need to be supported in their efforts for further professional development through adequate offers and resources.

To promote the quality of academic training in career guidance and counselling, NICE provides common reference points for all types of training for career practitioners. We aim to establish European competence standards to support the academic training of career practitioners, the mutual recognition of relevant degrees, and the quality assurance of career guidance and counselling programmes, mirroring the current challenges in societies, labour-market needs and the latest knowledge from different academic disciplines that underpin career guidance and counselling.

Competence-based training programmes are needed as learning opportunities for (future) practitioners to develop knowledge and skills, but also more general competences, values and attitudes in the role of active learners. To this end, training programmes need to be based on coherent concepts that integrate the acquisition of research-based knowledge with practical

---

[1] The NICE Memorandum was endorsed by the members of NICE at the sixth NICE Conference in Bratislava. The members of the steering committee and the network coordinators edited the text (in alphabetical order): Jean-Pierre Dauwalder, Bernd-Joachim Ertelt, Andreas Frey, Johannes Katsarov, Laura Nota, Hazel Reid, Christiane Schiersmann, Salvatore Soresi, Rie Thomsen, Raimo Vuorinen and Peter Weber. Facilitated by Peter Weber, all NICE partners were involved in the process of writing the memorandum, and 200 stakeholders had the opportunity to discuss the first version at the Canterbury Summit (09/2014).

training through innovative teaching and learning methods. Sufficient time and resources are prerequisites for this type of high-quality training for learners and teachers alike.

In line with the relevant UN declarations, training programmes in career guidance and counselling should promote the inclusion of all citizens to participate fully in society, education and work.

To strengthen the scientific basis of training, universities offering study programmes in career guidance and counselling should aim to establish a chair for career guidance and counselling.

Cross-border mobility should be an integral part of such training programmes in order to facilitate new cultural perspectives and the acquisition of innovative approaches for academic staff, students, practitioners and scholars.

INNOVATIVE RESEARCH AND EXCELLENT DOCTORAL TRAINING

To live up to its full potential, research in career guidance and counselling needs to increase its scope, enabling career guidance and counselling to be acknowledged as a distinct discipline. As an emerging discipline, research in career guidance and counselling needs to draw from the knowledge of various established disciplines, following an interdisciplinary approach. Correspondingly, established disciplines need to be informed about innovative perspectives, which arise through dedicated research on career guidance and counselling.

To achieve substantial progress in our research, we propose to form and foster lively research clusters through which we exchange appropriate research methodologies for career guidance and counselling, and develop and test new and effective models for career guidance and counselling.

Towards this objective, actual research needs and themes related to career guidance and counselling ought to be described in a broad interdisciplinary research agenda. A jointly developed research agenda, informed by issues relevant from the view of practitioners, policy and research will enable researchers to provide accessible, effective and high quality input for practice. We call upon the scientific community in our field to establish and develop further scientific formats of knowledge and information sharing.

To achieve sustainable progress in research and to enhance practice in our field, we need to ensure high quality doctoral training specialised on career guidance and counselling supporting novice scholars, especially through collaboration across higher education institutions from different countries and disciplines.

JOINT VENTURES OF RESEARCH, PRACTICE AND POLICY

We invite all actors involved in career guidance and counselling, practitioners, service users, policy makers, professional associations, research and training organisations to engage in intensive collaboration and exchange.

To improve the quality of career guidance and counselling and to make its potential more visible, we call for concrete actions: The practices and policies related to career guidance and counselling can be informed by evidence from research and vice versa. Such a research-based practice needs to be matched by practice-oriented research.

We strive to engage practice in research by involving practitioners, users and organisations as co-researchers in the research processes, including the definition of research questions. All scholars in our field are asked to engage in a strong and positive contact with the community of practice, organisations and networks. In particular, we will seek to establish opportunities for practitioners and groups of citizens to share their knowledge and to feed it into future practice, policy and research.

Last but not least, we will promote the professionalization of career guidance and counselling through high quality academic training, innovative research and active collaboration with all relevant stakeholders, especially those who represent vulnerable and marginalised groups.

We view the relationship between theory, research, policy and practice as central in the development of effective career guidance and counselling.

To achieve these goals, sustained international collaboration and exchange of research and training institutions is needed.

1

INTRODUCTION

Whether you read this handbook from the beginning or directly jump to the chapters, which interest you most, we hope you will discover many arguments, concepts and models, which can support your practice. All chapters will be relevant for our main target group, comprising managers, coordinators and lecturers engaged in the academic training of career practitioners. However, we believe that many of the contents presented in this volume will also be of interest for career practitioners, researchers, policy makers, representatives of professional associations and managers of career services. We suggest for you to read the introduction to decide, which chapters will be of particular interest to you.

In this chapter, you will find an introduction to the purpose and structure of this handbook. The introduction also offers an overview of the key concepts and terminology with which we will be working. An acknowledgement of the many people and organisations, who contributed to the results presented here, can be found at the end of the handbook, together with a map of the partners.

1.1 Purpose of the Handbook

The main purpose of this handbook is to introduce common European Competence Standards for the academic training of career practitioners[1] in Europe, together with some proposals and examples, of how to implement and establish such competence standards in practice. This overarching purpose directly relates to three main actions specified in the **NICE Memorandum** at the beginning of this volume. In particular, the European Competence Standards shall support the establishment of high quality, competence-based academic training for career practitioners in Europe. Furthermore, we hope that the competence standards will help to promote excellent doctoral training in our field.

Career guidance and counselling (CGC) is the fixed term[2], which we have decided to use in our network, when referring to the professional field, which we deal with. Both "career guidance" and "career counselling" are important and widespread terms used for referring to our field worldwide in research, study programmes and policy-making – at least in English language, where two such terms exists. In Europe, "lifelong guidance" has become another important expression, which stresses that citizens of all ages should be able to access career guidance and counselling. We acknowledge that there are disputes about the right terminology for the phenomena and practices, which we deal with in this handbook. If we have chosen to work with the most widespread terms, then not to take sides in this debate, but for our work to have a common starting point. The central practices, which we associate with career guidance and counselling, are the NICE Professional Roles, which we present in Chapter 3. They comprise Career Counselling, Career Education, Career Assessment and Information, Social Systems Interventions and Career Service Management and have been defined in NICE (2012), drawing on existing definitions and competence frameworks.

When we speak of **career practitioners**, we mean all people involved in the provision of career guidance and counselling, whether they do so as full Career Professionals, in addition to their primary occupation in another field (as Career Advisors), or in some kind of specialist function (as Career Specialists). We present our typology in Chapter 3.

When we speak of **competences** in this handbook, we are talking about a specific educative concept, which builds a link between the more detailed types of learning outcomes for academic training and the requirements of the labour market (see Chapter 4). In our understanding, acting with competence means that someone is able to meet complex demands in fulfilling a typical professional task. To act with competence, it is necessary to have particular knowledge, values, attitudes and skills. However, on their own, certain skills (e.g. active listening) or pieces

---

[1] Definitions of the words marked in blue at the beginning of chapters, can be found in the NICE Glossary at the end of the handbook.

[2] We realise that it is difficult to translate terms like career guidance and counselling into other languages. We kindly ask you to interpret them in a way, which suits the customs and culture of your context.

of knowledge (e.g. decision-making theories) will be insufficient to qualify someone for performing a professional task competently.

The ultimate purpose of academic training in career guidance and counselling should be to prepare people to support citizens dealing with career-related challenges in the most effective way. This calls for **competence-based learning**, which begins by asking the question, which real-life challenges career practitioners will need to be able to deal with in practice. Unlike only gathering theoretical knowledge through their studies, students are supposed to learn how to apply their knowledge, when, and for what sake. In the words of the European Qualifications Framework, competence-based learning is about ensuring that students develop an appropriate degree of autonomy and responsibility for their future practice (EQF 2008, p. 13).

A shared understanding about the competences needed by career practitioners has been a central question for NICE since our network was founded in 2009. In 2012, we succeeded in publishing our first set of **common points of reference (CPR)** for the academic training of career practitioners in Europe, the NICE Professional Roles, the NICE Core Competences, the NICE Curriculum Framework and the NICE Glossary. These CPR have already proven useful for many partners of the NICE community (and beyond). Several examples for how they have been used are illustrated in Chapters 6 and 7 of this handbook. The CPR published in NICE 2012 have helped establish a common agreement on the central roles of career practitioners in our contemporary societies. Additionally, they have helped to integrate different disciplinary perspectives in the development of study programmes, and offered a broad overview of relevant pieces of knowledge, professional values and attitudes, and skills, which may be relevant in the training and assessment of career practitioners.

With the second volume of the NICE Handbook, we take our work on common points of reference further, in agreeing on **European Competence Standards (ECS)**. By **competence standards**, we mean a shared agreement about the minimum level of competence needed to perform particularly important tasks in the field of career guidance and counselling. Competence standards define a common threshold in terms of the competences required for a particular practice: competences, which should be measurable in terms of a predefined quality level of practice.

The ECS will help to assure the quality of training for career practitioners around Europe and can support the mutual recognition of qualifications and prior learning in the field of career guidance and counselling. Additionally, they will support the professionalization of career guidance and counselling in terms of defining a common professional identity for career practitioners in Europe.

- On the one hand, the ECS shall contribute to assuring the quality of training for **Career Professionals**, who fully dedicate themselves to the practice of career guidance and counselling, e.g. as employment counsellors, career coaches, career counsellors or educational counsellors. In consideration of the growing challenges, which citizens

- face throughout their career development, the availability of professionals, who are prepared to offer exactly the support, which people need, is becoming more and more important (NICE 2012, Chapter 2).

- On the other hand, the ECS shall also contribute to assuring the quality of training for people who offer career support alongside their main occupation, whom we call **Career Advisors**. For the development of lifelong guidance systems in Europe, it is of central importance that other professionals, including teachers, social workers, HR managers and psychologists, can offer basic career support at a reliable level of quality, and judge when someone will benefit from working with a career professional.

- Thirdly, we have defined complementary competence standards for different specialisation routes in career guidance and counselling. The aim is to ensure that different types of **Career Specialists**, including trainers, managers and supervisors of career practitioners, as well as people conducting research and development in the field or evaluating career services, are competent to live up to their specific challenges. For the professionalization of career guidance and counselling, it is important for us to establish a common body of knowledge in Europe and to identify state-of-the-art practices and models, which can be mainstreamed through multipliers. This calls for us to also pay attention to further training offers for Career Professionals, when we think of standards for academic training.

It is important for us to stress that the European Competence Standards, which we propose in this volume are aspirational. We aspire to professionalise the practice of career guidance and counselling in the future. We want a trend towards good career services for all citizens in Europe, and see the necessity for a general up-skilling of people working in our professional field – no matter at which level of the system they operate. This will necessarily take time and effort. Therefore, we call for all relevant individuals and organisations to commit themselves to adopt the suggested competence standards gradually, and to take necessary actions to live up to the standards in the future.

The opposite of what we wanted to achieve through our work was a minimum compromise, where the European Competence Standards (ECS) only confirm that everything is fine the way it is and nothing needs to change. The way we have formulated the ECS, they will challenge everyone involved in the provision of career guidance and counselling and relevant training to engage in lifelong learning and further development. If we want career guidance and counselling to be respected as a profession in the future, and to become an acknowledged field of academic training and research all over Europe, we will all need to contribute.

The ECS are a voluntary framework. There are no formal legal obligations for their introduction. The primary users of the ECS will be higher education institutions, which offer qualifications in career guidance and counselling. With the ECS, we challenge ourselves as the providers of degree programmes in career guidance and counselling to review our curricula and the competences, which our graduates shall develop. In addition, we invite all other providers of relevant degree programmes, who were not involved in the project of working out the ECS to join us.

The ECS do not replace national qualification standards and benchmarks for career guidance and counselling. To enhance links and transparency in Europe, NICE calls on bodies in charge of national qualification frameworks for career practitioners, as well as national guidance forums and professional associations, to relate their standards and benchmarks to the ECS.

Frameworks like competence standards should be reviewed frequently, so that they can be adapted to technological developments, new trends and developments, and promote evidence-based innovation. It is our explicit ambition to revise the competence standards in the coming years and to continue working on them in the future. We realize that professional associations, policy-makers and national guidance forums, as well as other important stakeholders, have only been able to contribute to the development of the ECS as participants of the European Summit in Canterbury (2014) and the following public consultation. It is our ambition to involve stakeholders, and particularly career practitioners more actively in the further development of the ECS in the future. We kindly ask all interested actors to contact us, so we can include you in the next review.

The main purpose of this handbook is to support the implementation of the ECS and the other common points of reference, which NICE offers for academic training in career guidance and counselling. To support this purpose, this handbook offers advice for the interpretation of the competence standards. Furthermore, we recommend adequate qualification levels for the training of career practitioners, based on the ECS, and explain them in detail. Additionally, we deal with the question, which role the common points of reference can play for the quality assurance and quality enhancement of degree programmes and offer numerous examples, of how they are already being used in Europe for different purposes. Finally, to support cooperation at the European level and the implementation of the common reference points, we present a peer learning approach.

1.2 STRUCTURE

Chapters 2 to 5 present the European Competence Standards (ECS) in detail. We have conceived these chapters as an entity and the same group has edited them to ensure a high degree of coherence. Chapters 6 and 7 are dedicated to the use of NICE's common points of reference (CPR) for the quality assurance and enhancement of degree programmes, particularly through the approach of peer learning. Two distinct groups from the network have authored these chapters. Therefore, the style of these chapters is somewhat different from the prior chapters. All chapters are held together by the ambition to establish common competence standards for the training of career practitioners in Europe, maintain academic cooperation in Europe and assure the quality of higher education in our area.

Chapter 2 starts out by elaborating the different goals and challenges behind the development of the ECS. The chapter elaborates a variety of perspectives in doing so, considering needs for the quality assurance and professionalization of career guidance and counselling, the needs of higher education institutions and the labour market for career practitioners. The chapter closes by explaining how we designed the ECS, based on these goals and considerations.

Chapter 3 introduces a new concept, which we have developed over the past years: The NICE Types of Career Practitioners. A key conclusion from our analysis of the labour market for career practitioners has been the need to differentiate between three types of career practitioners, when defining competence standards for career guidance and counselling. In Chapter 3, we present this typology, culminating in the description of three distinct task profiles for Career Advisors, Career Professionals and Career Specialists. These task profiles draw on the NICE Professional Roles, which we also present as part of this chapter, along with some revisions since their first publication in 2012.

Chapter 4 presents the European Competence Standards (ECS) and explains the nature of measurable competence descriptions. In short, the ECS describe competence standards for the academic training of Career Advisors, Career Professionals and Career Specialists. For quick reference, please find the competence tables on pages 56-57. A short version is also available in different languages via www.nice-network.eu. At the end of the chapter, we explain how the ECS can be used for purposes of curriculum development. Here, we offer several examples for the interpretation of single competence standards. Additionally, we explain how the ECS can be used in combination with the NICE Curriculum Framework (NICE 2012).

Chapter 5 presents our recommendations for the qualification levels, at which academic training for different types of career practitioners should be offered. We have elaborated these recommendations based on the tasks profiles and the necessary competences of Career Advisors, Career Professionals and Career Specialists. For reference, we have worked with the *European Qualifications Framework for Lifelong Learning* (EQF) and the *Framework for Qualifications of the European Higher Education Area* (Bergen 2005, Appendix 1).

Chapter 6 discusses how the common points of reference (CPR) from NICE, including the ECS, can come into play when assuring and enhancing a programme's quality, e.g. in the revision of module handbooks, in the choice of trainers, or in the evaluation of degree programmes. Quality assurance refers to the process of ensuring that a new programme of study is fit for purpose. Many aspects of quality assurance are relatively formal, e.g. the preparation of a degree profile and curriculum, the selection of teaching, learning and assessment methods etc. Quality enhancement necessarily needs to follow and usually takes more informal actions in improving the quality of a degree programme. Several examples from NICE partners are offered to illustrate how the use of CPR can look in practice.

Chapter 7 goes on to introduce peer learning as a complementary method to the formal quality assurance procedures described in Chapter 6. Peer learning is a specific approach to foster innovation and excellence in degree programmes through the involvement of specialists from other degree programmes in quality assurance and enhancement activities. Case studies of peer-learning activities for quality development in the NICE community are presented along with guidelines for peer learning. The chapter also describes critical success factors and offers good examples of peer learning from within the NICE network.

At the end of the handbook, readers will find the **NICE Glossary**, which offers definitions for the terms, which we used in a standardised way. All terms marked in blue at the beginnings of chapters can be found in this glossary. The purpose of the glossary is to systemise all of the common points of reference and ensure the coherence and consistency of the underlying concepts and terminology.

2

GOALS AND DESIGN OF THE EUROPEAN COMPETENCE STANDARDS

In 2012, NICE published common points of reference, including the NICE Professional Roles, the NICE Core Competences, the NICE Curriculum Framework and the first version of the NICE Glossary (NICE 2012). The European Competence Standards (ECS), which we now propose for the academic training of career practitioners, build on these common reference points and take them a step further.

This chapter starts out by explaining what competence standards are and how the development of the ECS builds on prior achievements of NICE (Chapter 2.1). Then we offer a detailed account of the goals, which we pursue in issuing such competence standards as a European academic network (Chapter 2.2). In the conception of the ECS, we considered relevant needs and structures concerning quality assurance in career guidance and counselling, the labour markets for career practitioners and the functioning of higher education systems in Europe (Chapter 2.3).

To finalise the chapter, we present our conclusions for the design of the ECS (Chapter 2.4). In short, we conclude that the competence standards need to be linked to the typical tasks of career practitioners. For this purpose, tasks should be deducted from the NICE Professional Roles, which describe the societal mission of career guidance and counselling. However, we also come to the conclusion that different task profiles and competence standards are needed for different types of career practitioners.

2.1 Background[1]

The common points of reference, which NICE published in 2012, have already proven to be quite useful for many partners of the NICE community. The NICE Professional Roles, NICE Core Competences and NICE Curriculum Framework are being used for purposes such as setting up new degree programmes, developing existing programmes, organising new courses, reviewing national qualification benchmarks etc. (see Chapters 6 and 7 for detailed examples).

It is important for us to stress that the European Competence Standards (ECS) are firmly grounded on the common points of reference from NICE 2012. The NICE Professional Roles (NPRs) offer us a common understanding of the societal mission of the career guidance and counselling profession, of career services and career practitioners – across Europe and across different sectors of service provision (private, public, non-profit). The value of the NICE Professional Roles is that they offer a description, which is wide enough to capture the diversity of practice in our field, and narrow enough to agree that all career practitioners should be able to perform in each of the roles "to a greater or lesser extent" (NICE 2012, p. 43).

We will keep on referring to the NICE Professional Roles in this publication. However, the European Competence Standards (ECS) will replace the NICE Core Competences (2012) from now on. The NICE Core Competences served us as a first general agreement about the training needs of career practitioners in terms of competences, particularly in the form of the more detailed descriptions of "sub-competences" (NICE 2012, pp. 56-57). With the ECS, we offer an answer to the open question, what each career practitioner should be able to do "at least". We have taken the idea of competences further and agreed on a set of measurable competence standards.

Competence standards go beyond a shared agreement about the professional roles and tasks, which all career practitioners in all European countries should be prepared for. Competence standards also include an educative dimension and focus on the ability of practitioners to fulfil their roles and responsibilities. Competence standards offer a common framework of descriptions, *what* somebody should be able to do in order to fulfil particular tasks, and *how good* they should be able to do it, in order for them to be considered competent.

What is behind this difficult definition will become increasingly clear through the following chapters. However, it should become clear from this definition of competence standards that we have no ambition to "standardise" academic training in career guidance and counselling. Our goal is to quality-assure academic training in Europe through a shared framework of expectations regarding the competences of graduates.

---

[1] Chapter 2 has been prepared by Johannes Katsarov, Jukka Lerkkanen, Jacques Pouyaud and Kestutis Pukelis (in alphabetical order), who coordinated the development of the European Competence Standards (ECS) from 2013 to 2015, supervised through the NICE Steering Committee, and actively involving more than 50 experts from all across Europe at various workshops, conferences and online activities.

2.2 Goals

There are numerous goals for developing and establishing shared competence standards for the academic training of career practitioners at the European level. To reach these goals, the European Competence Standards (ECS) need to fulfil a number of quality criteria, which we considered in the development process.

1. The ECS shall help to establish career guidance and counselling as a recognised profession around Europe, by offering the basis for a common professional identity of career practitioners.

Only when citizens, institutions and career practitioners themselves have a common idea about "what career practitioners do", will our profession really be recognised and appreciated across Europe. For this reason, our framework begins with the question, what people should be able to expect from career practitioners. Our starting point needs to be a clear picture of the professional roles and task profiles of career practitioners.

2. The ECS shall help to assure the quality of training for career practitioners around Europe and support the mutual recognition of qualifications and prior learning in the field of career guidance and counselling (CGC).

The fundamental question that needs to be addressed in securing the quality of training for any profession is whether people are ready to tackle the challenges of the particular roles and tasks, which are associated to the profession. In other words, people need to be competent to perform in their job. For this purpose, it is necessary to have particular knowledge, particular values and attitudes, and particular skills, which together constitute the basis for a particular competence (Mulder et al. 2009). On their own, certain pieces of knowledge or skills are insufficient to qualify someone for filling out a professional role or performing a professional task competently. For this reason, the concept of competences is particularly important. Competences need to be defined as part of occupational descriptions for different types of career practitioners: They focus on the roles and tasks, which professionals shall perform, and link questions of knowledge, values, attitudes and skills to their overall meaning for the performance of practitioners.

Competence-based training, which focuses on preparing students for the challenges, which they will face in practice, increases the meaningfulness of degree programmes. It gives the design of the curriculum direction and helps in selecting teaching, learning and assessment methods, which support the development of competences. By actualising the curricula of degree programmes based on common competence standards, quality assurance can be taken a step further. Students can rely more strongly on learning what they will need to be able to do. Likewise, citizens, clients and employers can rely on the fact that the people offering career services have trained to become career practitioners in line with a widely acknowledged competence profile. This reinforces the professionalization of career guidance and counselling and contributes to assuring the quality of career services.

Useful competence definitions are rigid and measurable, and relate directly to the successful performance of a particular role or task. Only when they are measurable, they will also support competence-based assessment, and the competence-based recognition of prior learning. Finally, measurable competence standards increase the credibility of degrees awarded in other countries, increasing the mutual recognition of certificates and degrees internationally (Bergsmann et al. 2015).

3. The ECS shall help to foster innovation and international cooperation in the training for career practitioners around Europe.

In particular, the ECS should be able to support and foster:

- Shared concepts and guidelines for the training of career practitioners around Europe, e.g. concerning aspects of teaching, learning and assessment,
- Joint international training activities for students and practitioners of career guidance and counselling, both in terms of virtual courses and international events,
- A harmonised recognition of prior learning in Europe relating to competences and assessment instruments, award criteria and certificates,
- An increased international exchange of students between degree programmes dedicated to career guidance and counselling, building on enhanced comparability and transferability of credits,
- Enhanced international mobility of career practitioners, due to the availability of a joint framework for acknowledging qualifications in career guidance and counselling,
- The increased exchange of trainers from dedicated degree programmes, and
- Improved cooperation between higher education institutions and professional associations in linking entry-level training with continuous professional development.

The key element of the present work is then to build competence standards as vehicle for professionalization, allowing two-way transportation between defined occupational CGC activities and learning outcomes.

2.3 Challenges

From a political perspective, the validity and relevance of the European Competence Standards (ECS) need to be widely acknowledged around Europe – not only in academic circles, but also by career practitioners, policy-makers and citizen representatives. Therefore, it is particularly important for the ECS to build on the achievements of prior work done in this field internationally, and in various countries at the national level. As a tool for the enhanced convergence of academic training programmes in Europe, it is additionally of very high importance that a large number of degree programme providers from across all of Europe approve of them.

The major challenge in developing the ECS field was the need for a multilevel model, which is (1) relevant for the labour markets for career practitioners, which (2) fits the functioning of higher education systems, and which (3) fosters the (further) quality assurance and enhancement of career services and the professionalization of the career workforce. If competence standards are to be accepted in practice, used in training, and contribute to a higher quality of service provision, they need to add value in relation to the logics of each system. None of these three dimensions may be neglected, as we will show in the following. Integrating these different perspectives is one of the ways through which NICE wants to bridge existing gaps between research, training, practice and policy, as stressed in the NICE Memorandum (pp. 11-13).

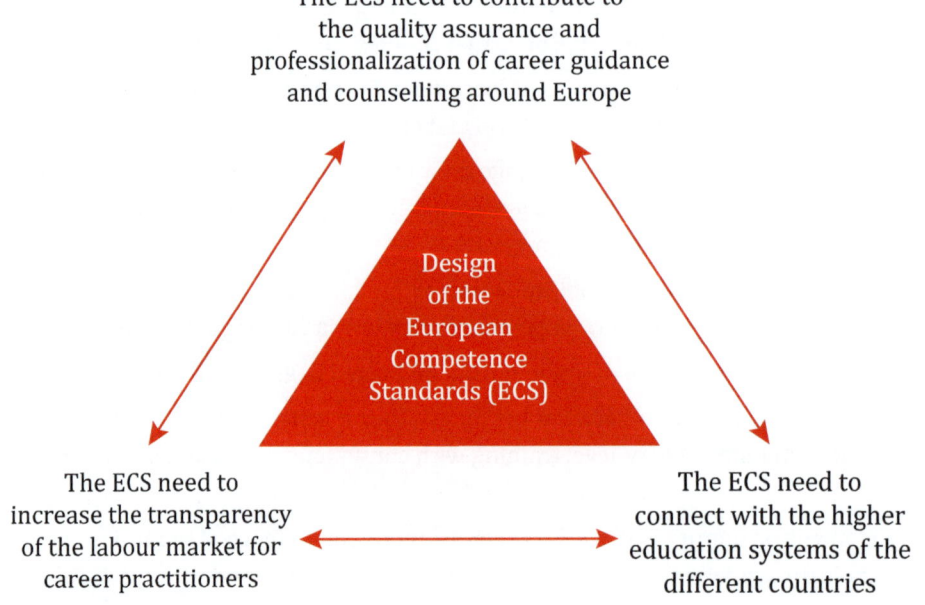

Figure 1: Three relevant dimensions for the design of the ECS, all rights reserved

The ECS need to contribute to the quality assurance and professionalization of career guidance and counselling around Europe.

The availability of lifelong guidance for all citizens, which is good enough to support them in mastering their career-related challenges, is still more of a political vision, than an actual reality. At the same time, multiple developments (globalization, aging populations, technological developments and growing specialisation of vocations, and the individualization of career decisions – to name only a few) increase the complexity of people's career-related challenges. In the future, we will not only need more career services and career practitioners to address these developments: in particular, we will need to secure the quality of career services and their relevance for addressing the needs of the population.

The quality assurance of career guidance and counselling is heavily dependent on the competence of practitioners. Schoolteachers, for instance, can certainly offer basic career support to their students, if they can draw on some specialised training. However, many career-related challenges, which people of all ages face, call for people who are trained as full Career Professionals. Due to multiple factors pertaining to the situation of citizens, including their abilities, their interests and their social context, Career Professionals need to develop custom-designed solutions for complex problems together with their clients (NICE 2012, p. 22). This calls for a high level of competence in a range of activities covering Career Counselling, Career Assessment & Information, Career Education, Social Systems Interventions and Career Service Management (the NICE Professional Roles). It also calls for a very broad, multi-disciplinary knowledge basis, which includes a strong understanding of individuals' motivation, learning and development, the functioning of organisations and communication, and the mechanisms of educational systems and the labour market, among others (NICE 2012, pp. 63-81).

For academic training in career guidance and counselling, the need for a larger and more professional career workforce means a growing political responsibility in Europe, which we have to acknowledge. For policy-makers and practitioners the implications are similar: we need to work together more closely in the future and jointly invest into a further development of career guidance and counselling. For a movement towards increasingly good and accessible career services, our starting point should be the actual career services and the existing training opportunities around Europe. We will look at the functioning of these systems next.

The important point that we need to keep in mind for the development of our framework here is that ECS should support the movement towards the professionalization of career guidance and counselling. It would be irresponsible for us to set standards, which all of us can already meet, only for the sake of pleasing everybody. Instead, we need to challenge ourselves to become better and prepare for the challenges of the future. In formulating competence standards, we need to concentrate on the question, what support citizens need – not what support they already get.

The ECS need to increase the transparency of the labour market for career practitioners.

In career services, where quality depends strongly on the competence of the career practitioner (NICE 2012, p. 22), clients and employers heavily rely on certificates, in choosing with whom to work (in addition to recommendations). It is difficult for people not specialised in career guidance and counselling to judge whether a degree in International Management, Developmental Psychology or Adult Education qualifies somebody to support them or their clients in facing career-related challenges. Similarly, there is still a lack of transparency and comparability concerning non-academic accreditation and certification schemes.

The ECS will add a value for the labour market for career practitioners, if they increase the transparency and comparability of relevant qualifications – in particular, concerning entry-level qualifications for practice. The competence concept is very useful for increasing the transparency and comparability of degree certificates, because it indicates, which professional roles and tasks a graduate is prepared to deal with in practice. When degree certificates can draw on international standards in the formulation of the competences of graduates, the transparency and comparability of relevant qualifications increase even more.

A particular challenge in defining competence standards for career practitioners is eminent all over Europe though. It concerns the question, who we are talking about, when we speak of career practitioners (Sultana 2009, pp. 23-24). Different types of practitioners are involved in the provision of career guidance and counselling in Europe, and we need to consider this diversity, when defining the ECS.

As we have stressed above, we see a need for dedicated Career Professionals, who are specialised on career guidance and counselling, and are competent in performing all of the NICE Professional Roles to some degree (NICE 2012, pp. 17-26). Nevertheless, we also need to acknowledge the findings of Watts and van Esbroeck (1998), whose analysis of guidance and counselling in the field of higher education has shown that many career-related challenges can be dealt with through what they call "first-in-line advisers". This relates to people who primarily work in another profession (e.g. as teachers), but who are capable of offering some amount of support in career-related questions, in addition to their primary roles and tasks. We recognise the value of such Career Advisors and the need of adequate training offers for them. However, we conclude that the training needed to practice as a full Career Professional goes far beyond what can be learned as part of a degree programme for another profession (e.g. as part of teacher training).

Furthermore, a European-level study from 2009 has demonstrated that there is additionally a need for some highly trained career practitioners, who are capable of performing very complex tasks, e.g. coordinating career services at regional or national levels, and conducting large-scale research projects (Cedefop 2009). We acknowledge the need for such Career Specialists, and adequate training offers. However, we conclude that some tasks expected from them would go far beyond the tasks that should reasonably be expected from all Career Professionals.

The ECS need to connect with the higher education systems of the different countries.

Following the philosophy of the Tuning programme, we assume that "universities don't look for uniformity in their degree programmes or any sort of unified, prescriptive or definitive European curricula but simply for points of reference, convergence and common understanding" (Tuning 2008, p. 6). The purpose of the ECS is certainly not to define one archetypal degree programme in career guidance and counselling (CGC) to be standardised all over Europe; neither through "ideal" Bachelor, nor through "ideal" Master programmes. The large variety and diversity of degree profiles in CGC is a rich indicator of the adaptability of our professional field. All existing programmes arguably focus on specific professional challenges, which may differ more or less; depending on the institutional structures of the different nations, the challenges, which different economies and labour markets face, political and organisational priorities etc.

We neither find it realistic (achievable), nor favourable to standardise the academic training in CGC all around Europe. Instead, we want to establish a set of minimal expectations across Europe, in terms of what career practitioners should be able to do. The ECS obviously must not represent "an ideal curriculum". They should encourage both variety and specialisation while promoting a common basis. Whatever model of competence standards we propose – there is no "one size fits all". Instead, we need a framework, which helps us to raise the quality of training in all of Europe, which enables more mobility and cooperation in Europe, but which respects the diversity and autonomy of higher education institutions and nations in line with the principles of the Bologna 2020 agenda (Leuven / Louvain-la-Neuve Communiqué 2009). Therefore, the ECS need to offer a flexible framework, which encourages the development of customised degree programmes, and which offers a common core at the same time. It should enable the mutual recognition of degrees and quality assurance of academic training in career guidance and counselling, but be adaptable for local contexts.

To enable the translation of qualifications between national systems and frameworks, the ECS will also need to relate to the *European Qualifications Framework for Lifelong Learning* (EQF 2008) and the *Framework for Qualifications of the European Higher Education Area* (Bergen 2005, Appendix 1). In particular, this makes it necessary to express how the ECS relate to the three cycles of academic training (Bachelor, Master and Doctorate), which are being harmonised across Europe through the Bologna process. They also need to live up to scientific standards regarding general advances in the quality of academic training. With the Bologna reform, there is a trend for harmonising the educational systems towards a higher degree of student-centred training. This calls for competence-based learning, which focuses on the readiness of graduates for their roles and responsibilities as professionals and citizens of an open and pluralistic society. Therefore, the ECS should be aligned with the principles of the EQF, particularly with its definition of competence and the level descriptors, which it offers for the domain of competence.

2.4 Design of the Competence Standards

Based on our goal to define measurable competence standards, and the strategic considerations explained above, we have concluded that we need to describe the concrete occupational challenges (tasks) of career practitioners in order to identify relevant competences needed to perform these tasks.

1. **Tasks** explain to the public what career practitioners actually do in practice. The purpose of task descriptions is to offer a clear idea about a person's job, which is also understandable for laypersons. **Task profiles**, which comprise several tasks, are used in human resource management to define the occupation of an employee or a category of employees.

2. **Competences** are important for purposes of training and assessment of people's readiness to perform tasks at an agreed quality level. When formulated as **learning outcomes**, competences offer measurable descriptions of what a person should be able to do, e.g. as a professional or a citizen. They therefore provide goals for education and training, which relate to concrete challenges that people will face as citizens and professionals.[2]

The identification of the typical tasks of career practitioners legitimises the definition of relevant competences. Therefore, we have decided to develop task profiles for career practitioners, based on which we can define the European Competence Standards. Task descriptions of professionals need to be justified in terms of how they fit into the societal mission of the particular profession. For the purpose of defining the societal mission of the career guidance and counselling profession, we have developed the NICE Professional Roles (NICE 2012).

3. **Professional Roles** define the broader societal expectations associated with a particular profession. They provide professionals and their clients with a basic idea about the profession. The **NICE Professional Roles (NPRs)** together represent what we consider to be the professional roles of career practitioners across Europe. To live up to their societal mission, all career practitioners should be able to perform in each of the NPR to a greater or lesser extent. Full Career Professionals should additionally consider all of them as part of their professional identity.

Therefore, we have concluded that the task profiles should be derived from the NPRs. This implies splitting the NPRs into more concrete task descriptions, based on which we can define the competence standards. Each task should mark one particular activity, which states a central aspect of each career practitioner's task profile in Europe.

---

[2] For competences to become suitable for purposes of education, training and assessment, they can be broken down into more easily measurable types of learning outcomes, as we will see in Chapter 4.

However, a key conclusion from our analysis has been the need to differentiate between **three types of career practitioners**, when defining competence standards for career guidance and counselling. Distinct minimum competence standards should be defined for Career Advisors, Career Professionals and Career Specialists.

Hence, our approach is to develop **distinct task profiles** for each of these three types of career practitioners. Drawing on the NPRs, we have ensured that the tasks of each group are central for the practice of career guidance and counselling. Additionally, we conceived the three types in such a way that they would build on each other in terms of competence development and the conception of possible qualification pathways. Therefore, the tasks of the three different types are arranged in such a way that an increasingly wide and distinct competence profile is expected, when moving from basic practice (Career Advisors) to the performance of a Career Professional, and from there to the performance of highly specialised tasks (Career Specialists).

For the definition of the competence standards (based on the individual tasks), we employ **level descriptors**, through which the competences become measurable (in terms of a defined quality level of performance). For the purpose of increasing the transparency and comparability of qualifications in career guidance and counselling, we connect the competence standards with references to the *European Qualification Framework for Lifelong Learning* (EQF 2008). This allows us to make recommendations for the appropriate levels of academic training of the different types of career practitioners, based on the central tasks they shall perform in practice.

Three Types
of Career Practitioners

As explained in Chapter 2, the explication of concrete tasks of career practitioners is a necessary step towards the definition of European Competence Standards presented in Chapter 4. The aim of this chapter is to introduce three types of career practitioners, along with distinct task profiles.

The chapter begins with the introduction of the NICE Professional Roles (NPRs), which we have revised since their first publication in 2012. The NPRs represent the widest and most recent consensus in Europe relating to the societal mission, for which career practitioners should be prepared. Therefore, they are fundamentally important for understanding and defining task profiles for the three types of career practitioners. The NPRs are presented in an updated version, followed by explanations for the revisions (Chapter 3.1).

Next, we offer a general introduction of the NICE Types of Career Practitioners (Chapter 3.2). We explain how the different types of career practitioners relate to each other and examine the need to define competence standards for each type. Finally, we present distinct task profiles for each type of career practitioner (Chapter 3.3). The lists of tasks, which we present, reflect the work of many international and national organisations regarding the professional challenges of career practitioners. They also form the direct reference for defining European Competence Standards in the following chapter.

3.1 THE NICE PROFESSIONAL ROLES REVISITED[1]

The NICE Professional Roles (NPRs)[2] together represent what we consider the professional roles of career practitioners across Europe. They offer a broad definition of the central roles and responsibilities of career practitioners. To live up to their societal mission, all career practitioners should be able to perform in each of the NPRs to a greater or lesser extent (NICE 2012, p. 48).[3] Each of the NPRs is important for the practice of career guidance and counselling (CGC). In Figure 2, this is symbolized through a large circle, which unites the five roles as central aspects of the CGC profession.

The large circle around the NPRs is our first innovation of the framework: In the version from 2012, there were six roles, and the central role was that of the "CGC Professional". It was placed in the middle of the other five roles, which lead to many misunderstandings: many readers thought that we were talking about six distinct job profiles, which exist independent from each other. The new model stresses that the professional practice of career guidance and counselling (large circle) involves and integrates five roles. What we used to call the central role ("CGC Professional"), was in fact a professional identity as a career practitioner, which incorporates different roles.

A second important revision, which goes in the same direction, is that we have decided to speak of the roles in a more activity-oriented way. In 2012, we spoke of the "Career Counsellor" and "Career Educator" roles, for instance. We now speak of the Career Counselling and Career Education roles instead, to avoid misunderstandings. Career practitioners should not only be prepared to perform what we call Career Counselling, or Career Education. They should be able to select an adequate role for their activities, based on the needs to their clients, and combine the different roles in meaningful ways.

Figure 2 illustrates the five professional roles of career practitioners. Career practitioners can switch between these professional roles at work, sometimes combining them, sometimes focusing on a particular role.

---

1 Chapter 3 has been prepared by Johannes Katsarov, Jukka Lerkkanen, Jacques Pouyaud and Kestutis Pukelis (in alphabetical order), who coordinated the development of the European Competence Standards (ECS) from 2013 to 2015, supervised through the NICE Steering Committee, and actively involving more than 50 experts from all across Europe at various workshops, conferences and online activities. The NICE Professional Roles (NPRs) and the NICE Types of Career Practitioners (NTCPs) are open educational resources, and form a joint accomplishment of the members of NICE. Provided the source is acknowledged, they may be distributed freely. Translations are available on www.nice-network.eu

2 When speaking of "roles" we refer to the sociological understanding of "social roles as clusters of expectations that are attached to people's behaviour in a particular society, in regard to one of their positions" (Dahrendorf 1958, p. 144; Schimank 2007, p. 47).

3 With the distinct task profiles for three types of career practitioners, we propose minimum expectations in terms of the extent to which Career Advisors, Career Professionals and Career Specialists should be able to perform the NPRs in practice (see Chapter 3.3).

Figure 2: The NICE Professional Roles, Open Educational Resource: NICE 2016

- **Career Counselling** describes the professional role of career practitioners to support people in making sense of the situations they are experiencing, working through issues towards solutions, making difficult career decisions, and realising personal change.

- **Career Education** describes the professional role of career practitioners to support people in developing their career management competences, i.e. the competences, which they need for career-related learning and development.

- **Career Assessment & Information** describes the professional role of career practitioners to support people in attaining relevant information about themselves (e.g. their interests, talents and competences), the labour market, and educational or vocational options – depending on their individual information needs.

- **Social Systems Interventions** describes the professional role of career practitioners to support people and organisations in designing and developing adequate career pathways.
- **Career Service Management** describes the professional role of career practitioners to manage and assure the quality of their work.

To explain the NICE Professional Roles (NPRs) in more detail, we will comment on each of them in the following. We will also explain changes, which we have made since the first version of the NPRs in 2012.

Career Counselling

Career Counselling builds on a strong professional relationship. It allows clients to open up to new possibilities, rethink themselves and their role in society. It is in this role that career practitioners support their clients in understanding their situations and formulating goals for career development etc. In this sense, it is also in the Career Counselling role that career practitioners motivate clients to engage in learning (Career Education) and draw on different sources of information when making decisions and plans (Career Assessment & Information). Due to this role's centrality, we argue that Career Guidance and Counselling is a "counselling profession" – at least, when it is practised professionally.[4]

Career Education

Career management competences include the ability to become aware of own resources and needs, understanding the functioning of labour markets, vocational and educational systems, the mature use of career information systems, developing career plans, making career decisions, adapting to change pro-actively, self-presentation skills etc. Career Education can take place as part of Career Counselling, e.g. when career practitioners train their clients to use reflective methods in such a way that they will be able to use them autonomously in the future. Career Education can also take place in terms of special training sessions, e.g. in teaching groups how to assess their competences and interests and make career plans.

Career Assessment & Information

Career Assessment & Information should always be client-centred; therefore, it begins with the assessment of people's informational needs, before specific techniques and resources are used to provide information, which is relevant in the individual case.[5] Career Assessment &

---

[4] Professional practice of career guidance and counselling refers to the work of Career Professionals (see Chapter 3.2). Career Advisors only practice career guidance and counselling next to their primary occupation.

[5] We have therefore changed the order of "information" and "assessment" in the role's title.

Information should only be exercised in combination with the Career Counselling role. This is necessary to make sure that Career Assessment & Information is relevant and meaningful for the client, and that the new information is reflected upon appropriately.

Social Systems Interventions

Careers are always embedded in social systems, so the structures and cultures of society, organisations and institutions are immensely important when it comes to individuals' potentials for career development. Social Systems Interventions support individuals, organisations and political communities alike, when it comes to making social systems more inclusive, efficient and effective. For instance, it includes supporting clients in entering an organisation (placement), or improving cooperation between public services and employers for the promotion of inclusion and social justice. Social Systems Interventions also include the moderation of career-related conflicts between clients and their relatives, employers or educators, including advocacy for clients who face discrimination.[6]

Career Service Management

The management of career services (including Career Education, Career Assessment and Information, Career Counselling, and Social Systems Interventions) requires a good understanding about how career services work, how their quality can be measured and secured, and what kind of support different types of clients need. In particular, customising career services to clients' individual needs demands a high level of autonomy of career practitioners and career services. For precisely this reason, management must be considered an integral part of the practitioners' identity.[7]

3.2 The NICE Types of Career Practitioners

Our analysis in Chapter 2.3 demonstrates that we need three different sets of competence standards. The practice of career guidance and counselling (CGC) doesn't only involve five professional roles, in which career practitioners support people. It is also necessary to distinguish between people who offer basic career support next to their primary professions, professionals, who are fully dedicated to career guidance and counselling, and people, who offer highly

---

[6] In 2012, this role was titled "Social Systems Intervener & Developer". We have removed the aspect of "development" from this role, since the focus on promoting organisational change went beyond what could be expected from a normal career practitioner, who concentrates on working with individual clients.

[7] In 2012, this role was called "Programme & Service Manager". This led to many misunderstandings, since "Programme & Service Management" seemed too general for it to be considered a professional role of career practitioners. Since the role concentrates on the management of career services, which can also include programmes and projects, we have renamed it to "Career Service Management".

specialised services related to CGC. Therefore, we have developed competence standards for each of these three types of career practitioners: Career Advisors, Career Professionals, and Career Specialists.

1. **Career Advisors** are important sources of basic information and support for people facing career-related challenges. Career Advisors are teachers, placement managers, psychologists, social workers or public administrators (among others). They are not Career Professionals, but professionals in another field, who offer some career support in addition to their primary roles and tasks. Often they are the first persons to whom people come for advice. They should be able to offer basic support and advice at a reliable level of quality and immediately understand when a person would benefit from professional career services. These tasks come with a significant responsibility, which is why we argue that Career Advisors should undertake academic training based on specific competence standards.

2. **Career Professionals** are dedicated to career guidance and counselling and see it as their vocation to support people in dealing with complex career-related challenges. They include career counsellors, employment counsellors, career coaches, school counsellors, personnel developers, educational or guidance counsellors (among others). Career Professionals need to be ready to support people who are facing uncertainty, multi-faceted problems and unpredictable situations, knowing that their career decisions could have a heavy impact on their lives. They support the development of strategic approaches, offer access to highly specialised knowledge, and help clients in facing stressful phases of transition and projects of personal change.

3. **Career Specialists** are specialised in one (or more) of the five professional roles and work towards the advancement of CGC in different ways. Some of them concentrate on practical matters, e.g. the management of career services, policy-making or the supervision of career practitioners. Others primarily engage in research and development or academic training in CGC. In addition to their ability to practise as Career Professionals, Career Specialists need to demonstrate substantial authority, scholarly and professional integrity in a particular area of career guidance and counselling.

All three types of career practitioners are of particular importance for quality assurance in the provision of career guidance and counselling. To make the relevance of all types of career practitioners concrete, we created a solar model (Figure 3). It demarks the relationship of Career Advisors, Career Professionals and Career Specialists to the client. The solar model symbolizes the importance of all types of career practitioners to clients and stresses that all types of services must be accessible for clients, depending on the career-related challenges they are dealing with.

Figure 3: Interrelation of the three types of career practitioners, Open Educational Resource: NICE 2016

With the introduction of distinct task profiles and competence standards for Career Advisors, Career Professionals and Career Specialists, NICE responds to demands from diverse policy-makers, professional bodies and other experts to differentiate between different types of career practitioners. In the following, we will shortly present some of our main arguments:

Distinction between Career Advisors and Career Professionals

There is an obvious need to differentiate between Career Advisors and Career Professionals. If we only gave Career Professionals a clear profile, Career Advisors would not feel valued in their important role in society, or they might feel overburdened with the high expectations connected with the competence standards of the Career Professional profile. On the other hand, it would be unacceptable for Career Professionals to have their task profiles and competence standards limited to what other professionals can offer in addition to their primary roles and tasks in another profession.

Additionally, there are no common concepts, which kinds of competences schoolteachers need when it comes to career questions. Likewise, it would be helpful to offer a suggestion for the minimum competences, which those people working in public employment services should have, who frequently need to decide, whether somebody would benefit from career guidance and counselling, or not. As long as basic training in career guidance and counselling is not part of the standard training curriculum for other professionals, who might be asked for career support, it makes sense for NICE to define this kind of a profile.

Distinction between Career Professionals and Career Specialists

The reasoning behind distinct task profiles and competence standards for Career Specialists is inherent in the need to professionalise career guidance and counselling. Professionalization goes beyond putting career professionals in charge of practice in terms of self-management (Evetts 2011, p. 13). It includes the development of specialised academic training, and the development of self-regulative governance structure for professional practice, including the definition of shared professional and ethical standards (Schiersmann & Weber 2013, p. 48).

An important question is which competences the people need, who train or supervise Career Professionals and Career Advisors. Moreover, we could ask which competences the people need, who manage large career services. Due to the complexity of career guidance and counselling, we argue that the coordination and supervision of career services should be driven by Career Professionals – not by people with little or no understanding of the roles and tasks of career practitioners (NICE 2012, 23 ff.). However, leading and managing large career services, e.g. regional teams of more than 20 career counsellors, will require competences, which go beyond what can be expected of all Career Professionals. Therefore, we suggest that a distinct pathway for specialisation in career guidance and counselling should concern Career Service Management.

Finally, as the NICE Memorandum (pages 11-13) stresses, establishing an academic discipline and large-scale research activities in the field of career guidance and counselling requires people, who are competent for interdisciplinary, practice-oriented research. In view of the complexity of career services, highly specialised people are needed, who will be able to take research and development forward in the field, drawing on an intimate understanding of the actual challenges in practice.

Promotion of Professional Mobility

Last but not least, the distinction between three types of career practitioners promotes professional mobility. It promotes vertical mobility within the profession, as it defines routes for career progression: A person can enter the field having trained as a Career Advisor. Drawing on this training, a qualification as a Career Professional becomes more accessible. For Career Professionals, different options of becoming Career Specialists are defined, which comprise a broad diversity of options. Horizontal mobility will be promoted by making the field more accessible through training options as Career Advisors, which can be offered for many different professionals, e.g. social workers. Different Career Specialist roles also connect with other professions, e.g. supervision, evaluation, or academic training. Horizontal mobility is also promoted between different "counselling professions" through the framework. It helps to clarify, which additional competences would be expected from psychological counsellors, or organisational consultants, who want to practise as Career Professionals.

3.3 Task Profiles

As a basis for the definition of competence standards, we need a framework of tasks, which describe the concrete challenges and activities of career practitioners in an understandable way. Due to the need to differentiate between three types of career practitioners, we have defined distinct task profiles for Career Advisors, Career Professionals and Career Specialists. Task profiles, which comprise several tasks, are used in human resource management to define the occupation of an employee or a category of employees.

The NICE Professional Roles offer a strong framework, based on which tasks profiles can be identified, since they describe the broader areas of activity of career practitioners (Chapter 3.1). When we defined task profiles for career practitioners based on the NICE Professional Roles, we were guided by the analytical question: "What do Career Advisors/Career Professionals/Career Specialists do in this professional role?" Some of the tasks, which we identified, are relevant for several roles, which is why we define them in an additional category called generic professional tasks. This means that they are important for all of the professional roles.

For a comprehensive collection and definition of the most central tasks of the career guidance and counselling profession, we consulted a large variety of literature, including:

- A European Reference Competence Profile for PES and EURES Counsellors (PES to PES 2014),
- Degree programme descriptions from various countries, including proposals for BA and MA level programmes from the EU-project DICBDPEC (2013),
- A systematic comparison of several international and national competence frameworks (Katsarov et al. 2012), including the international competence frameworks of the IAEVG (2003) and CEDEFOP (2009), and
- The descriptions, which we had already jointly developed in in NICE (2012), including the NICE Professional Roles and the relevant task profiles.

In defining the task profiles of the three types of career practitioners, we also ensured that the tasks would build on each other consecutively to enable vertical mobility of learning and career development:

- The tasks of the Career Advisors are very basic, so that they could be included as an additional module in training programmes for other professionals, e.g. teachers, or be offered in terms of further education for other professionals.

- The tasks of Career Advisors also belong to the portfolio of Career Professionals. This makes it easier for people who are already qualified as Career Advisors to train as Career Professionals. Additionally, the task profiles of Career Professionals comprise all of the tasks, which professional practice of career guidance and counselling requires across Europe for a large variety of target groups.

- The tasks of the Career Specialists all rely on a qualification as a Career Professional. This ensures that Career Specialists are identified as members of the profession, even if they have specialised themselves in one or more of the professional roles, and do not necessarily practice as Career Professionals.

3.3.1 Task Profile of Career Advisors

Career Advisors are people who clients with career-related questions often approach first. We have proposed that Career Advisors will have a partnering role for Career Professionals and a supportive role regarding career-matters. Career Advisors are teachers, placement managers, psychologists, social workers or public administrators (among others). Their professional tasks related to career guidance and counselling (Figure 4) are only part of one of the diverse roles of Career Advisors, who primarily identify themselves as members of another profession than career guidance and counselling.[8]

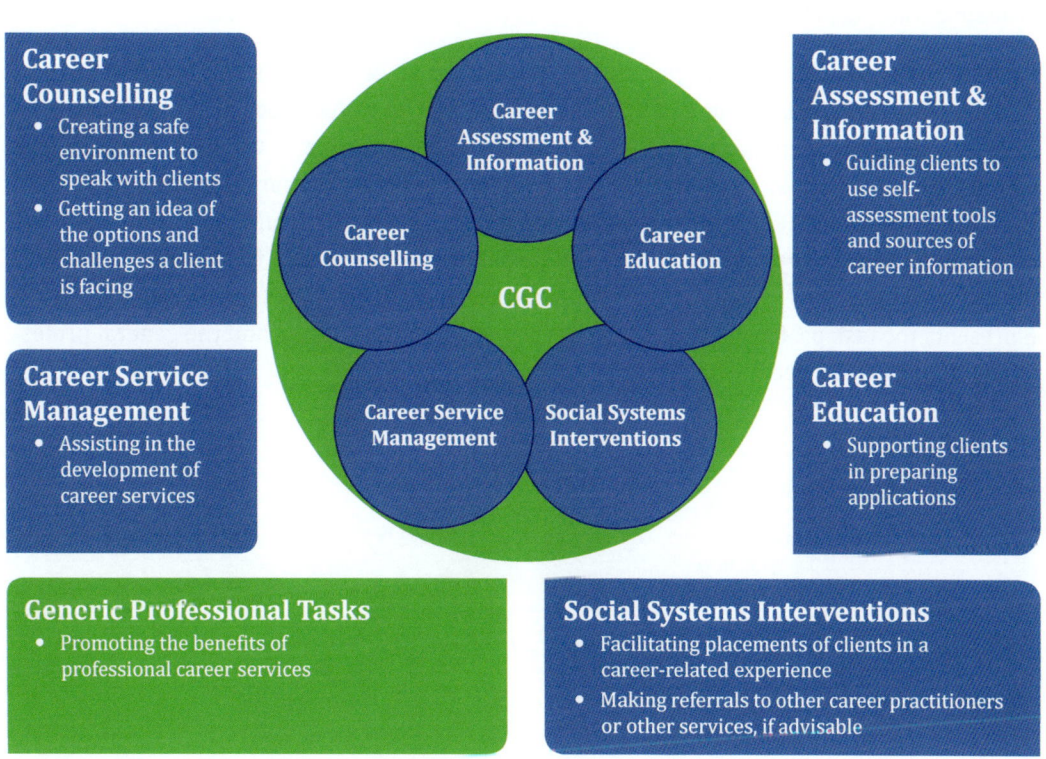

Figure 4: Task Profile of Career Advisors, Open Educational Resource: NICE 2016

---

8   Examples of occupations, which could match this profile: School teachers, university lecturers, professional trainers, social workers, psychotherapists, placement specialists, recruiters, HR managers, rehabilitation specialists.

3.3.2 Task Profile of Career Professionals

Career Professionals are the people, who are dedicated to career guidance and counselling and who see it as their vocation to support people in facing complex career-related challenges through Career Counselling, Career Education, Career Assessment & Information, Social Systems Interventions and by managing their career services professionally. Their task profile (Figure 5) also includes all of the tasks of Career Advisors.[9]

3.3.3 Task Profiles of Career Specialists

Career Specialists are specialised in one (or more) of the five professional roles and work towards the advancement of career guidance and counselling in different ways. Some of them concentrate on practical matters, e.g. the management of career services, policy-making or the supervision of career practitioners. Others primarily engage in research and development or academic training in CGC.

Some of the tasks of Career Specialists are relevant for all of them. We characterize them as generic professional tasks. For example, we believe that all Career Specialists, whether working as a researchers, managers or policy makers, should be able to train the professionals whom they work with. Additionally, we define distinct tasks for Career Specialists for each of the NICE Professional Roles, as areas of specialisation. Therefore, to offer an example, a Career Specialist, who is specialised on Career Counselling should be able to perform the generic professional tasks plus the tasks defined for "Career Specialists in Career Counselling". Figure 6 presents the task profiles of the different types of Career Specialists and the general professional tasks of all Career Specialists.[10]

---

9 Examples of occupational titles, which could match this profile: Career counsellor, school counsellor, career coach, guidance counsellor, employment counsellor, personnel developer, educational counsellor.

10 A few examples of occupations, which could match this profile, if the particular profile focuses on career guidance and counselling: Professors, university lecturers, researchers, supervisors, specialists in ministries, specialists in regional administration, specialists in public employment services (PES), coordinators of career services, managers of career centres, organisation developers, quality controllers and evaluators, consultants.

Career Assessment & Information

- Guiding clients to use self-assessment tools and sources of career information
- Identifying informational needs of clients
- Providing clients with relevant information and sources of information, including assessment tools
- Investigating clients' interests and resources

Career Education

- Supporting clients in preparing applications
- Facilitating basic learning about general educational and vocational options
- Assessing clients' career management competences
- Facilitating learning for clients to improve their career management competences

Social Systems Interventions

- Facilitating placements of clients in a career-related experience
- Making referrals to other career practitioners or other services, if advisable
- Developing and coordinating interdisciplinary networks to draw on helpful connections in case clients need additional support
- Advocating on behalf of clients to promote their career development when they face strong opposition or social constraints
- Mediating career-related conflicts

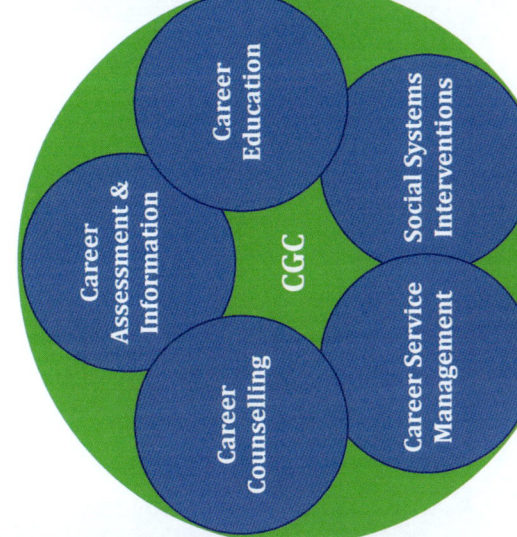

Generic Professional Tasks

- Promoting the benefits of professional career services
- Engaging in continuous reflection and development of their own practice
- Dealing with role and value conflicts effectively

Career Counselling

- Creating a safe environment to speak with clients
- Getting an idea of the options and challenges a client is facing
- Supporting clients in clarifying their career-related goals, needs, options and challenges within their life contexts
- Building constructive counselling relationships
- Supporting clients in tackling challenging projects of personal change and coping with transition phases
- Supporting clients in the interpretation of complex situations
- Supporting clients in exploring options, making and implementing career-related decisions

Career Service Management

- Assisting in the development of career services
- Marketing career services for particular target groups, including outreach to marginalized groups
- Coordinating own work effectively and efficiently
- Building partnerships with clients and other professionals
- Assuring the quality of their work according to standards and target-group needs

Figure 5: Task Profile of Career Professionals, Open Educational Resource: NICE 2016

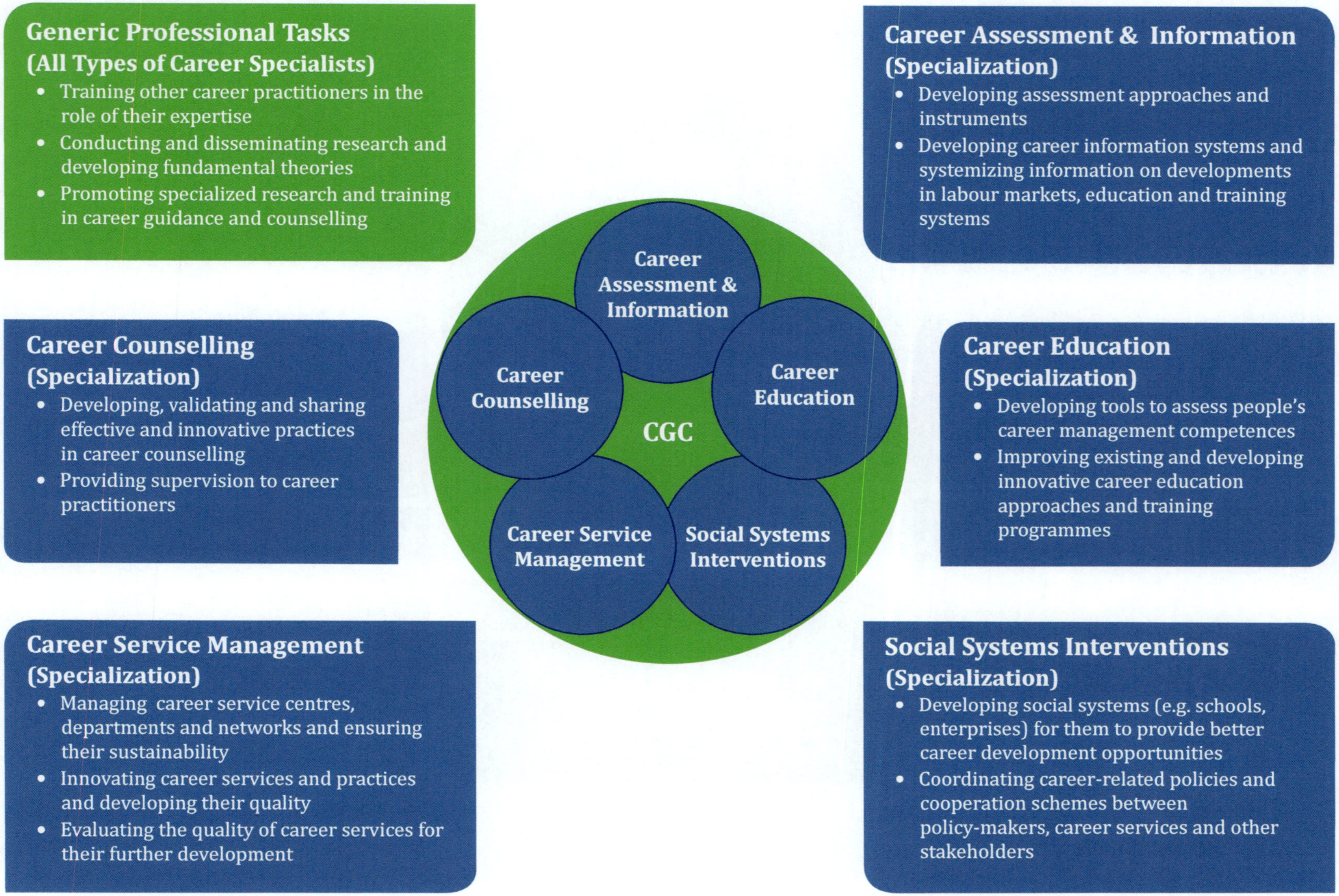
Generic Professional Tasks
(All Types of Career Specialists)
Training other career practitioners in the role of their expertise
Conducting and disseminating research and developing fundamental theories
Promoting specialized research and training in career guidance and counselling
Career Assessment & Information
(Specialization)
Developing assessment approaches and instruments
Developing career information systems and systemizing information on developments in labour markets, education and training systems
Career Counselling
(Specialization)
Developing, validating and sharing effective and innovative practices in career counselling
Providing supervision to career practitioners
Career Education
(Specialization)
Developing tools to assess people's career management competences
Improving existing and developing innovative career education approaches and training programmes
Career Service Management
(Specialization)
Managing career service centres, departments and networks and ensuring their sustainability
Innovating career services and practices and developing their quality
Evaluating the quality of career services for their further development
Social Systems Interventions
(Specialization)
Developing social systems (e.g. schools, enterprises) for them to provide better career development opportunities
Coordinating career-related policies and cooperation schemes between policy-makers, career services and other stakeholders
Career Assessment & Information
Career Counselling
Career Education
CGC
Career Service Management
Social Systems Interventions

Figure 6: Task Profile of Career Specialists, Open Educational Resource: NICE 2016

4

EUROPEAN COMPETENCE STANDARDS

NICE articulates the need for European Competence Standards (ECS) for the qualification of three types of career practitioners: Career Advisors, Career Professionals and Career Specialists. The distinct task profiles of these three types of career practitioners have been introduced in Chapter 3.

From the perspective of NICE, increasingly high levels of competence are necessary for people to fulfil the professional roles and tasks of these three types of career practitioners. For this reason, NICE formulates competence standards at these three consecutive levels of practice in career guidance and counselling. NICE stresses the need for each of these three groups to engage in specialised academic training as an entry requirement for their type of practice in career guidance and counselling. Due to the high level of autonomy and responsibility required for each type of practice in career guidance and counselling, NICE also pronounces the need for all career practitioners to engage in continuous professional development and lifelong learning.

The European Competence Standards are a voluntary framework. There are no formal legal obligations for their introduction. NICE encourages all higher education institutions offering qualifications in career guidance and counselling to relate their degree programmes to the ECS. This will allow us to reach the goals formulated in Chapter 2.

This chapter introduces the ECS. To begin with, our understanding of competence is explained (Chapter 4.1). Building on this definition, we explain how the ECS have been formulated based on task descriptions (Chapter 4.2). Chapter 4.3 presents the ECS in the format of a table, beginning with a brief description of the table's system. Following the presentation of the ECS, we explain how they can be interpreted for the purpose of developing the curricula of degree programmes in career guidance and counselling (Chapter 4.4). Here, we also clarify how the NICE Curriculum Framework from 2012 can be connected with the ECS. Questions relating to qualification levels are discussed separately in Chapter 5

4.1 Competence Definition[1]

When we speak of competence standards, we share a distinct understanding of what competences are in NICE, drawing on the competence definitions offered in the European Qualifications Framework (2008) and by the OECD (2003). We define a **competence** as the ability of a person to meet complex demands in particular situations, drawing upon adequate psychosocial resources in a reflective manner (NICE 2012, p. 32). We would like to highlight several aspects of our competence definition explicitly, since it differs from popular understandings of competence to some degree:

From our understanding, a competence is a particular type of **learning outcome**, i.e. a statement about what learners know, understand, and are able to do upon completion of a particular learning process (ECTS Users' Guide 2015). Through the description of learning outcomes, degree programmes and qualifications are supposed to become understandable, comparable and measurable – a central goal of the Bologna Process (Pukelis 2011, p. 40).

Competences are the most sophisticated type of learning outcomes. A competence describes the ability of an individual to solve a particular type of real-world problems. In relation to professions and professional roles, competences are associated to the tasks of the particular professionals. Competences are about performing activities autonomously and responsibly, e.g. building a constructive counselling relationship with a client. Particularly when confronted with uncertainty, complexity, multi-faceted issues and unknown factors, competence requires creativity, critical thinking and a strategic mind-set. Competence also relies heavily on a reflective process, through which professionals make sense of a particular problem or situation and decide how to use their psychosocial resources in an adequate way, in order to arrive at a desired outcome.

By **psychosocial resources**, we refer to less complex types of learning outcomes, which form the basis of competence. They include knowledge, values, attitudes and skills. Individuals usually mobilise multiple psychosocial resources in dealing with complex challenges competently. For instance, knowledge could relate to a Career Professional's ability to draw on theories in working with a client, for example theories of career development, organisational change and labour-market logics. The professional's values and attitudes would be activated when valuing the client's involvement in and shared responsibility for the counselling process, for example. Relevant skills, which a career practitioner might mobilise while working with a client, could comprise interviewing techniques, analytical approaches or know-how in working with a career information database.

---

1 Chapter 4 has been prepared by Johannes Katsarov, Jukka Lerkkanen, Jacques Pouyaud and Kestutis Pukelis (in alphabetical order), who coordinated the development of the European Competence Standards (ECS) from 2013 to 2015, supervised through the NICE Steering Committee, and actively involving more than 50 experts from all across Europe at various workshops, conferences and online activities. The presented outcomes, the ECS, are Open Educational Resources, and form a joint accomplishment of the members of NICE. Provided the source is acknowledged, they may be distributed freely. Translations are available on www.nice-network.eu

4.2 Formulation of Competence Standards

For competence descriptions to be meaningful for academic training and for employment questions, they need to be measurable and prepare people for performing a particular task successfully. In Chapter 3, we have presented the NICE Types of Career Practitioners (Career Advisors, Career Professionals and Career Specialists) together with detailed task profiles. The tasks defined for each of these groups are the basis for the formulation of distinct competence standards for each type of career practitioners.

To reach the requirements of measurable and meaningful competences, we grounded our work on a performance-oriented definition of competences (Chapter 4.1). Furthermore, we applied taxonomies of educational objectives (Bloom et al. 1956; 1964), guidelines for developing measurable level descriptors (Moon 2002), and the level descriptors for the domain of competence offered in the European Qualifications Framework (EQF 2008).

Following Moon (2002, p. 64), a competence definition always includes three parts:

- A description of what a learner should be able to do at the end of a study process, using an action verb
- A word or words that indicate how a task is actually performed
- A word or words that indicate the conditions under which the activity is performed (e.g. expectations of clients, superiors, complexity of a problem etc.)

The three parts ensure that an observable behaviour (activity) is connected with the definition of a quality level (standard) of the performed activity. Here we need to describe a minimum threshold: the minimum acceptable behaviour for someone to be considered competent at the given level (Moon, 2002, p. 10). These **level descriptors** are defined by expressing how the activities are performed, the circumstances under which they are performed and/or which measurable outcomes are required. Similarly, the selection of the action verb also defines the quality level of the task, which shall be performed. For example, a different level of competence is need for "developing a career counselling approach" than for "applying a career counselling approach".

An important aspect in the definition of competences is that they should concentrate on offering criteria, which can be measured in an educational setting. In addition, the expectations and circumstances should apply to a multitude of typical professional situations, but still concentrate on what is most relevant. The following example illustrates how we defined one of the competence standards, following the principles, which we outlined above. We have selected one of the tasks of Career Professionals, which we view as relevant in all professional roles (generic professional tasks):

"Engaging in continuous reflection and development of their own practice"

This task description can be understood easily. Not only by career practitioners, but also by laypersons. However, it is far from measurable, and there is little indication of the level of quality, which is expected in terms of reflection and development. Contrarily, the respective competence standard formulates very explicit expectations:

"Review the process of one's own professional interaction with a client, in consideration of the client's needs, and professional and ethical standards for career guidance and counselling"

To begin with, the competence standard defines an observable behaviour. "Continuous reflection" is hard to observe, and reflecting "out loud" while working with a client would often be inappropriate in a real professional interaction. Therefore, the standard expects Career Professionals to be able to "review the process of [their] own professional interaction with a client". We suppose that somebody, who is able to reflect their practice, e.g. in the form of a case study, will also be able to reflect their practice while performing.

The competence standard goes on to raise explicit expectations in terms of how to review one's professional interaction with a client. The formulation concentrates on some of the most difficult aspects of professional reflection. On the one hand, it ensures that Career Professionals have to go into substantial detail in reviewing the professional interaction, since they are asked to "review the process". Additionally, Career Professionals are confronted with the expectation to consider needs of their clients as part of the analysis. This necessitates that they review the appropriateness and effects of their own actions throughout the process and explicitly consider the clients' needs while doing so.

Finally, the competence standard expects that Career Professionals will be able to conduct their review "on the basis of professional and ethical standards for career guidance and counselling". This expectation calls for a high level of reflective competence. On the one hand, the competence standard implies that Career Professionals should not only be able to memorise or understand professional standards and ethical codes. They should be able to use them for purposes of evaluation and self-assessment. On the other hand, the quality level also depends on the explicit reflection of professional standards and ethical guidelines, which are concerned with the practice of career guidance and counselling. This implies that practice must also be reflected from a more objective point of view, taking specific professional norms into account (not only one's own opinions).

Certainly, the discussion of this example cannot reflect all of the aspects, which we considered in the formulation of the competence standard. However, it demonstrates the logic behind the complex formulations.

4.3 The European Competence Standards

The European Competence Standards (ECS) take the shape of a table, which can be found on pages 56-57. Each competence standard corresponds to one of the tasks as defined for the three types of career practitioners in Chapter 3. The table forms a matrix of horizontal and vertical categories. To provide a good overview of the competence standards, the ECS for each type of practitioner are arranged in six horizontal categories of competences, which correspond with the NICE Professional Roles:

- Generic Professional Competences
- Career Counselling Competences
- Career Education Competences
- Career Assessment & Information Competences
- Career Service Management Competences
- Social Systems Interventions Competences

Vertically, we begin with the Career Advisor Competences at the top of the table. In the middle of the table, they are followed by the Career Professional Competences. The Career Specialist Competences can be found at the bottom. This arrangement corresponds with the increasingly specialised and complex tasks related to career guidance and counselling, which distinguish the three types of career practitioners described in Chapter 3.

This system also implies that Career Professionals should also have the competences expected of Career Advisors in order to perform their roles and tasks. Likewise, Career Specialists should be competent to practise as Career Professionals and as Career Advisors – independent of the professional role, in which they specialise themselves.

4.4 Using the ECS for Curriculum Development

The European Competence Standards (ECS) offer a relatively short list of measurable competence descriptions. This helps in offering a transparent and meaningful overview of central objectives for the academic training of career practitioners in terms of what they should be able to do in practice upon graduation.

The ECS only define standards at the level of competences (see Chapter 4.1). They do not define standards for more detailed types of learning outcomes in terms of knowledge, values, attitudes or skills. Setting standards at the level of more detailed learning outcomes is viewed critically, since it threatens the autonomy of higher education and is viewed as too prescriptive. Common standards at the level of competences offer a lot of room for adaptation and interpretation to the specific focus of a degree programme and its local context – therefore competence standards tend to be adopted more readily.

However, for the purpose of curriculum development and the conception of teaching, learning and assessment activities, more detailed learning outcomes than competences are needed. In this sub-chapter, we will deal with the question how the ECS can be interpreted for the purpose of defining more detailed types of learning outcomes. In general, learning outcomes can be used both for the purpose of defining the goals of teaching and learning activities and for identifying suitable assessment techniques.

The translation of competences into more concrete types of learning outcomes is a creative process, which requires a high level of expertise in the area of career guidance and counselling, in addition to didactical competence. It needs to integrate affective, behavioural and cognitive dimensions of learning, in order to foster the development of competences. Additionally, competent professionals may draw on different resources to solve an identical problem effectively. Very often, there are several viable approaches to success (Le Boterf 2014, p. 77). Competent practitioners should be able to choose among a variety of options in tackling typical challenges of their profession, thus being able to draw on a large variety of psychosocial resources.

For the interpretation of the ECS in the development and revision of curricula for study programmes in career guidance and counselling, we provide two examples in this section. These examples concentrate on the translation of the competence standards into more detailed learning outcomes and provide some ideas about the selection of adequate teaching, learning and assessment approaches. At the end of the sub-chapter, we shortly introduce the NICE Curriculum Framework (2012) as a resource, which can be used for this purpose.

4.4.1 EXAMPLES

Example 1: Concluding a client's main reason for seeking support

In our first example, we will look at the competence of Career Professionals to "conclude a client's main reason for seeking support in an empathic and respectful way, based on a client-centred interview" (Domain of Career Counselling Competences). The main focus of this competence is to assure that Career Professionals are ready and able to truly understand the needs and concerns of the people seeking their support.

Understanding and empathy only become observable through a verbalisation: Hence, the action verb "conclude". The action description already includes a quality level descriptor, since it focuses on the client's "main reason" for seeking support.

	Generic Professional Competences	Career Counselling Competences	Career Education Competences
Career Advisors are ready and willing to …	1. Assess potential benefits of career services for individuals, communities and organisations to better deal with existing and emerging challenges	1. Produce a confidential, respectful and supportive environment for clients to speak openly about their career-related concerns 2. Confirm the type of career-related challenge a client is facing, based on active listening to concerns and questions voiced by client	1. Explain how to prepare applications for jobs and training opportunities (CVs, letters, interviews) to the level of general standards 2. Explain how to learn about educational and occupational options and requirements, with reference to available resources for the specific target group
Career Professionals are ready and willing to …	1. Review the process of one's own professional interaction with a client, in consideration of the client's needs, and professional and ethical standards for career guidance and counselling 2. Develop strategies to overcome personal role and value conflicts while working with clients from different backgrounds, in alignment with professional and ethical standards for career guidance and counselling	1. Conclude a client's main reason for seeking support in an empathic and respectful way, based on a client-centred interview 2. Formulate an offer for a counselling agreement with a client, specifying objectives and approaches that suit the client's priorities and resources 3. Explore which psychological and external resources are available to support the client to cope with phases of stress and achieving personal growth 4. Assess complex life situations and different types of information together with clients, based on their interests, competences and other resources 5. Apply suitable models for problem solving, decision making and strategic planning, based on the interests and preferences of clients, as well as their resources	1. Assess the career management competences and learning needs together with clients, applying appropriate instruments and approaches 2. Design career education sessions, combining educational contents and methods to support members of a particular target group, with flexibility to respond to their specific learning needs and behaviours in the process
Career Specialists are ready and willing to …	1. Provide academic training to reach learning outcomes according to international and national quality standards to assure the competence of career practitioners 2. Conduct original research on career-related topics to inform evidence-based practice, rigorously applying scientific standards and principles of good communication 3. Justify the value of interdisciplinary research and training in the field of CGC based on the findings of various academic disciplines and empirical knowledge on the particular challenges of career services	1. Design career counselling approaches and instruments to support target groups with specific needs in solving their career-related problems, responding to verified demands of practice 2. Review the practice of career practitioners for the development of their competence and professional self-awareness in a collaborative way, paying particular attention to intercultural and ethical aspects	1. Develop methodologies for measuring people's career management competences for particular target groups, based on scientific methodology and verified demands of practice 2. Develop strategies, curricula and training programmes for improving the career management competences of a specific target group based on actual needs of the target group and relevant quality standards

Career Assessment and Information Competences	Career Service Management Competences	Social Systems Intervention Competences	
1. Identify websites, self-assessment tools and other sources which provide career information for the particular target group of the client, responding to the explicit interests, abilities, skills, competences and needs they have formulated	1. Report on the quality of career services based on specific quality criteria and standards for career guidance and counselling	1. Arrange a voluntary meeting of a client with a placement-provider, relating to the needs formulated by the client 2. Judge when to make a referral to a career professional or to another service, based on assessment of one's own ability to provide the support needed	Career Advisors are ready and willing to …
1. Assess informational needs of clients, regarding their interests and competences, the relevant labour market, and features of vocational and educational systems, to confront informational problems such as information overflow, stereotypes, disinformation, and lack of information 2. Select scientifically validated methods and tools for self-assessment, as well as information sources to satisfy the clients informational needs 3. Assess particular resources, interests or other relevant characteristics of an individual client using a suitable career assessment approach of high validity in a collaborative way, to provide the client with personally relevant information	1. Construct appropriate communication channels, language and arguments to attract members of a particular target group to a particular career service offer 2. Implement career services strategically in cooperation with other relevant actors to reach relevant target groups 3. Produce good professional relations with clients, colleagues and organisations to ensure quality of career services 4. Review career services and their organisation on the basis of quality standards for career guidance and counselling and the needs of their specific target groups, and propose viable approaches for service enhancement, based on such an analysis	1. Identify common interests between the perspectives of different stakeholders in supporting a particular target group (e.g. early school leavers), to propose how relevant cooperation structures could be built up and maintained (networking) 2. Justify a need for support and propose a strategy in the case of an individual client in dealing with relevant stakeholders (e.g. parents, employers, public institutions) for the sake of the client's career development 3. Devise recommendations on how to overcome a career-related conflict, based on a fair evaluation of the interests of all involved parties	Career Professionals are ready and willing to …
1. Design career assessment approaches and tools (tests, questionnaires, scales etc.), to provide a relevant and reliable diagnosis of people's career related interests, abilities, competences, motivations and other characteristics 2. Design career information systems to systemise relevant information on specific labour markets, education and training systems, and to anticipate emerging trends and issues, to suit the search patterns and interest of relevant target groups	1. Evaluate the quality of techniques and programme evaluation models used in career services, applying standards and expertise on innovative and effective practices 2. Appraise human resources of career services applying appropriate management approaches to ensure the quality and sustainability of career services provided, also in relation to funding 3. Implement a quality assurance and development system to secure relevant quality standards and improve the quality of services in a collaborative way with other stakeholders	1. Design concepts for more inclusive and effective social systems and their implementation in collaboration with employers, policy-makers and other stakeholders, based on an evaluation of the systems' ability to foster social justice, employment and the well-being of communities, organisations and individuals 2. Design policies and strategies for inter-sectorial and interdisciplinary coordination in cooperation with relevant stakeholders at regional, national or international level	Career Specialists are ready and willing to …

Table 1: European Competence Standards, Open Educational Resource: NICE 2016

Whether a Career Professional has concluded a client's main reason for seeking support can be verified with the client easily. This makes it possible to assess this competence in practice. For instance, clients could be asked to assess the degree to which their career counsellor understood their main reason for seeking support immediately after the initial interview. However, it is also possible to assess this competence by the means of recorded interviews. For instance, students could be shown a video of a career-counselling interview, as a basis for formulating their conclusion without the presence of a real client.

Further level descriptors of the competence standard concern the expectations that Career Professionals

- Conduct client-centred interviews to come to conclusions (fully concentrating on the client, not telling own stories etc.)
- Put themselves in the situation of their clients when formulating conclusions (demonstrating empathy)
- Treat their clients with respect, even if the clients are disrespectful of themselves

These three points are, of course, an interpretation of the competence standard, where we read that the conclusion shall be done "in an empathic and respectful way, based on a client-centred interview".

The level descriptors, which make the competence standards measurable, are the key to the translation of the ECS into more detailed learning outcomes and the identification of suitable teaching, learning and assessment techniques. A large number of learning outcomes can be deducted from this competence standard.

For example, conducting a client-centred interview requires (among others):

- theoretical knowledge about interpersonal communication
- knowledge about the reasons out of which people seek career support, i.e. an overview of the career-related challenges, which people might face
- understanding and applying the principles of a client-centred interview
- skills to build the trusting interpersonal relationship needed for such an interview
- skills to ask questions the right way
- a professional attitude characterized by empathy and interest in how the other person makes sense of her situation etc.

This account of relevant resources, which foster the competence of a prospective Career Professional to "conclude a client's main reason for seeking support in an empathic and respectful way", is surely not complete. However, it provides an impression of the types of learning outcomes, which need to be considered strategically in the training of Career Professionals.

Discussion

Obviously, some of these learning outcomes represent knowledge. There are many ways of developing knowledge, e.g. by reading relevant books and articles, through discussions and analysis. Relevant assessment could investigate, to which extent a learner is able to apply a particular theory in the analysis of a situation, for example.

Contrarily, the development of skills cannot only draw from theory, but must be practised. Relevant learning activities could be the application of particular interviewing approaches with fellow students and role games. However, a critical analysis of counselling interviews (e.g. recordings) can also help students to develop relevant skills. Assessment will typically follow similar lines.

The development of professional attitudes and values can be fostered in diverse ways, including through group discussions, or by learning about the effects of different behaviours (including unwanted and unethical behaviours). The assessment of values and attitudes is often integrated with assessment at the level of competence. Whether a Career Professional is empathic and respectful can be judged based on the way they conduct a client-centred interview, and on the way they formulate their conclusion for the "client's main reason for seeking support".

Example 2: Assessing the informational needs of clients

In our second example, we will look at another complex competence standard. While the task description seems quite simple ("Identifying informational needs of clients"), a competent Career Professional must be able to address a number of level descriptors in assessing a client's informational needs.

Concretely, Career Professionals are expected to be able to "assess informational needs of clients regarding their interests and competences, the relevant labour market and features of vocational and educational systems to confront informational problems such as information overflow, stereotypes, disinformation and lack of information" (Domain of Career Assessment and Information Competences).

The competence standard formulates level descriptors concerning:

1. the areas of knowledge, which a Career Professional must consider
2. the purpose of the assessment and necessary consequences
3. the informational problems, which a Career Professional must be able to detect

This example also demonstrates how the competence standards implicitly set standards concerning skills, professional attitudes and the knowledge of career practitioners. For instance, it is seen as the ethically appropriate behaviour to "confront informational problems" (professional attitude). Secondly, particular skills are necessary to confront specific informational problems, e.g. stereotypes, and ask the right questions to identify the problems in the first place. Finally, Career Professionals must be knowledgeable about the assessment of interests and competences (psychological and educational constructs, selection of appropriate assessment tools), labour markets, vocational and educational systems (economic theory, institutions, policies), and specific types of informational problems (e.g. stereotypes).

Discussion

This example displays the need for a multi-disciplinary knowledge basis as NICE recommends for the academic training of all people involved in the provision of career guidance and counselling. If Career Professionals should be able to confront a lack of information on the labour market, they need a good understanding of economics. Assessing whether available information overwhelms a client requires psychological knowledge.

Furthermore, the competence standard implies that Career Professionals need to be able to understand verbal and non-verbal cues of clients. The development of these kinds of skills again requires practice. For instance, people training as Career Professionals will benefit from learning formats like job shadowing, particularly when the trainee is involved in the reflection of career counselling sessions.

The development of appropriate professional attitudes, such as confronting informational problems will definitely benefit from a sound understanding of these types of problems (e.g. nature and development of gender stereotypes), but also from learning specific intervention techniques, e.g. circular questioning, from the study of role-models and practice.

4.4.2 WORKING WITH THE NICE CURRICULUM FRAMEWORK

A valuable resource, which supports the interpretation of the European Competence Standards (ECS) for purposes of curriculum design and development, is the NICE Curriculum Framework (NICE 2012, pp. 59-79). The NICE Curriculum Framework is composed of nine modules (see Figure 7). The modules systemise numerous ideas for the definition of learning outcomes in terms of competences and resource requirements. Additionally, each module proposes suitable approaches for teaching, learning and assessment, which can inspire curriculum development and design.

Three Knowledge Modules (K-Modules) make up the foundation of the NICE Curriculum Framework. They provide basic knowledge, which is important for the practice of all five NICE Professional Roles. In Figure 7, they form the "foundation of the temple". To organise the various pieces of knowledge, which are of general importance for the practice of career guidance and counselling, we differentiate between knowledge on:

- Individuals and Careers (Module K1)
- Organisations, Groups and Communication (Module K2), and
- Society, Politics and Markets (Module K3)

The five Competence Modules (C-Modules) correspond with the NICE Professional Roles Career Counselling, Career Education, Career Assessment & Information, Career Service Management, and Social Systems Interventions.[2] In Figure 7, they form the "pillars of the temple". In each of these modules, readers will find ideas for role-specific learning outcomes.

Three types of resource requirements are presented as part of the C-Modules. They refer to the psychosocial resources, which career practitioners shall develop as the basis of their competences for practice in career guidance and counselling. We define the three types of psychosocial resources as follows (NICE 2012, p. 38):

- **Cognitive resources** mainly reflect knowledge that people have and can use to find solutions to specific questions or problems. Cognitive resources go beyond information (who, what, when) and comprise the understanding of theories (why, how), i.e. assumptions on how different phenomena are connected with one another (causal relations).

- **Affective resources** are aspects that bring about the motivation and volition (willpower) of practitioners to do the right thing. They become visible through attitudes and behaviours, such as individual judgments people make, actions taken, ideas expressed and so on. Attitudes very strongly determine how people act and think and are strongly influenced by their values and societal norms.

- **Behavioural resources** are frequently referred to as skills. Skills differ from knowledge, as they are action-oriented and come for the experience of having done something before. The quality of skills is primarily based on the quality of knowledge and the amount of practice, which people have had in doing something, e.g. in the application of a particular technique or instrument.

The C-Modules are particularly helpful in translating the ECS into more detailed learning outcomes, since the resource requirements are directly linked to the corresponding NICE Professional Role. Through the broad diversity of learning outcomes, they help in keeping an overview of what relevant aspects of training could be.

---

2 We remind our readers at this point that the titles of some of the NICE Professional Roles have changed since 2012: "Career Information & Assessment" is now called Career Assessment & Information; "Programme & Service Management" has been renamed to Career Service Management; "Social Systems Interventions & Development" has been renamed to Social Systems Interventions. In NICE 2012, the modules carry different names than the ones presented here.

Finally, the Generic Professional Competences Module (P-Module) describes learning outcomes, which are important for the practice of all NICE Professional Roles, and which go beyond general knowledge (which can be found in the K-Modules). The P-Module corresponds with the domain of the Generic Professional Competences of the European Competence Standards. In particular, cognitive, affective and behavioural resources can be found here, which refer to professional ethics, dealing with complexity, reflective practice, research and analysis. In Figure 7, the P-Module forms the "roof of the temple" in analogy to the idea of the career guidance and counselling profession, which integrates the five professional roles, holds them together, and gives practice direction.

Figure 7: Modules of the NICE Curriculum Framework, Open Educational Resource: NICE 2016

In their combination, the European Competence Standards and the NICE Curriculum Framework bring together two aspects: common minimum standards for the training of different types of career practitioners on the one hand; and a broad and flexible framework, which encourages the development and comparability of customised degree programmes on the other hand.

5

Recommended Qualification Levels

To enhance links and transparency in Europe, NICE calls on bodies in charge of national qualification frameworks for career practitioners, as well as relevant professional associations, to relate their standards and benchmarks to the European Competence Standards (ECS) and to participate in the further development of the ECS.

The ECS do not replace national qualification standards and benchmarks for career guidance and counselling. They are a voluntary framework, so there are no formal legal obligations for their introduction. NICE encourages all relevant bodies to relate their standards and benchmarks to the ECS by 2018. This will allow us to reach the goals formulated in Chapter 2, namely promoting the professionalization and quality assurance of career guidance and counselling all across Europe, and fostering a strong basis for cooperation at the European level.

In this Chapter, we recommend qualification levels for the academic training of the three types of career practitioners, which we introduced in Chapter 3. We begin by presenting a short summary of our recommendations (Chapter 5.1). Due to the high competence requirements associated with career guidance and counselling, the ECS only relate to the academic qualification levels of the Framework for Qualifications of the European Higher Education Area (Appendix 1).

As a reference framework for our recommendations, we have worked with the European Qualifications Framework for Lifelong Learning (EQF 2008), which we introduce in Chapter 5.2. The EQF serves as a meta-framework and offers generic level descriptors for the assessment, which complexity of learning outcomes is adequate for eight qualification levels. In the following sub-chapters, we present our arguments for the recommended qualification levels for each type of career practitioner. We do so by analysing, with which level of the EQF individual competence standards from our framework correspond.

5.1 Recommended Qualification Levels[1]

NICE stresses the need for each type of career practitioner to engage in specialised academic training as an entry requirement to their type of practice. Based on our analysis of the European Competence Standards (ECS), we can only recommend the three **academic qualification levels** of the Framework for Qualifications of the European Higher Education Area (Bergen 2005) as a solid basis for the practice of career guidance and counselling. These three academic cycles correspond with Levels 6, 7 and 8 of the *European Qualifications Framework for Lifelong Learning* (EQF 2008). In the following, we present our key recommendations, before we explain them in detail in Chapter 5.2.

Our recommendations in terms of the **duration of academic training** are based on the *Framework for Qualifications of the European Higher Education Area* (Bergen 2005), which can be found in Appendix 1, and which endorses the ECTS system. Depending on the country, one ECTS point corresponds with 25-30 hours of study, and 30 ECTS points generally correspond with one semester of full-time studies (ECTS User's Guide 2015, p. 10).[2]

For the academic training and recognition of prior learning of **Career Advisor** competences, NICE recommends reference to EQF Level 6. Academic training could be as part of, or offered in addition to Undergraduate certificates and Bachelor-level programmes in diverse disciplines. Additionally, it could be offered as part of Postgraduate or Master-level degree programmes. Academic training for Career Advisors should also be accessible for people in vocational leadership positions, but should not be awarded at a lower level than EQF 5, which corresponds with short-cycle higher education offers (Bergen Communiqué 2005).

For the academic training and recognition of prior learning of **Career Professional** competences, NICE recommends full degree programmes at EQF Level 7, particularly specialised Master degrees or Postgraduate Diplomas. This implies that the duration of academic training for Career Professionals should amount to 1-2 full years of study at at Postgraduate or Master level (60-120 ECTS points). At the lowest, academic training should be offered in terms of specialised Bachelor programmes (EQF 6) of 3-4 years (180-240 ECTS points).

For the academic training and recognition of prior learning of **Career Specialist** competences, NICE recommends reference to EQF Level 8, e.g. as part of structured doctoral training. At the lowest, training should be provided in terms of specialised Postgraduate certificates or Master Degrees (EQF 7).

---

1   Chapter 5 has been prepared by Johannes Katsarov, Jukka Lerkkanen, Jacques Pouyaud, and Kestutis Pukelis (in alphabetical order). The presented outcomes form a joint accomplishment of the members of NICE.

2   ECTS stands for European Credit Transfer and Accumulation System. The purpose of the ECTS is to increase transparency and comparability between degrees of European member states. The use of this credit accumulation and transfer system also encourages the modularisation of degree programmes and generally aims at enabling more flexibility in higher education (e.g. in terms of learning mobility).

5.2 Elaboration of Recommended Qualification Levels

As a reference framework for assessing the qualification level needed for training people to perform particular tasks, we have applied the *European Qualifications Framework for Lifelong Learning* (EQF 2008), which defines eight qualification levels. Each of the levels offers generic level descriptors, which define the complexity of learning outcomes in terms of (1) knowledge, (2) skills and (3) competences, which would be adequate for this level of training. Of these eight levels, EQF Levels 5-8 are relevant for academic training in general and for the academic training of career practitioners in particular. Table 2 presents Levels 5-8 of the EQF (2008).

	Knowledge	Skills	Competence
Level 5	- comprehensive, specialised, factual and theoretical knowledge within a field of work or study and an awareness of the boundaries of that knowledge	- a comprehensive range of cognitive and practical skills required to develop creative solutions to abstract problems	- exercise management and supervision in contexts of work or study activities where there is unpredictable change review and develop performance of self and others
Level 6	- advanced knowledge of a field of work or study, involving a critical understanding of theories and principles	- advanced skills, demonstrating mastery and innovation, required to solve complex and unpredictable problems in a specialised field of work or study	- manage complex technical or professional activities or projects, taking responsibility for decision-making in unpredictable work or study contexts - take responsibility for managing professional development of individuals and groups
Level 7	- highly specialised knowledge, some of which is at the forefront of knowledge in a field of work or study, as the basis for original thinking and/or - research critical awareness of knowledge issues in a field and at the interface between different fields	- specialised problem-solving skills required in research and/or innovation in order to develop new knowledge and procedures and to integrate knowledge from different fields	- manage and transform work or study contexts that are complex, unpredictable and require new strategic approaches - take responsibility for contributing to professional knowledge and practice and/or for reviewing the strategic performance of teams
Level 8	- knowledge at the most advanced frontier of a field of work or study and at the interface between fields	- the most advanced and specialised skills and techniques, including synthesis and evaluation, required to solve critical problems in research and/or innovation and to extend and redefine existing knowledge or professional practice	- demonstrate substantial authority, innovation, autonomy, scholarly and professional integrity and sustained commitment to the development of new ideas or processes at the forefront of work or study contexts including research

Table 2: European Qualifications Framework for Lifelong Learning, EQF 2008

In relation to the *Framework for Qualification of the European Higher Education Area* (Bergen 2005, Appendix 1), the EQF Levels 5-8 relate directly to particular cycles of academic training (EQF 2008, p. 16):

- **EQF Level 5** learning outcomes correspond with the so-called "short cycle" of higher education, which takes place within the first cycle (Bachelor level), or linked with it. This follows the conception that Bachelor degree programmes typically require a Level 4 qualification for entry, but end with a Level 6 qualification. Some countries offer Undergraduate diplomas, which correspond with EQF Level 5.

- **EQF Level 6** learning outcomes correspond with the first cycle of higher education, which is mostly associated with Bachelor degrees.

- **EQF Level 7** corresponds with the second cycle of higher education, which is mostly associated with Master degrees or Postgraduate diplomas. These qualifications have in common that they usually require a Level 6 qualification for entry.

- **EQF Level 8** learning outcomes correspond with the third cycle of higher education, which is most commonly associated with a Doctorate. Typically, qualifications at EQF Level 8 demand a qualification at EQF Level 7 as an entry requirement.

To derive recommendations for the qualification levels of academic training for the NICE Types of Career Practitioners, we have consulted the EQF level descriptors, which we introduced in Table 2. Concretely, once we had formulated level descriptors for the tasks of the different types of career practitioners, we systematically linked the requirements with the EQF level descriptors. In the following sub-chapters, we will explain our recommendations from Chapter 5.1, offering several examples to explain our assessment, based on the EQF.

5.2.1 Career Advisors

Nine competence standards are formulated for the training of Career Advisors (see Table 1, pages 56-57). For the academic training and recognition of prior learning of Career Advisor competences, NICE recommends reference to EQF Level 6. Academic training could be as part of, or offered in addition to Undergraduate certificates and Bachelor-level programmes in diverse disciplines. Additionally, it could be offered as part of Postgraduate or Master-level degree programmes. Academic training for Career Advisors should also be accessible for people in vocational leadership positions, but should not be awarded at a lower level than EQF 5, which corresponds with short-cycle higher education offers.

The reason, why NICE recommends to offer qualifications for Career Advisors at EQF Levels 6 or Level 7, is that the profile of Career Advisors is suitable to be integrated into the postgraduate qualifications of "non-career professionals", e.g. teachers, social workers, HR managers etc. The qualification of Career Advisors will not fill a complete degree programme, since the profile is that of "a role next to others" – not of a vocation in itself. Based on a brief assessment of the Career Advisor competences, we assume that 15-30 ECTS points of training would be justified as a sufficient quantity of learning activities. This assumption needs to be verified through concrete research on available training programmes, their duration and the learning outcomes of their graduates though.

Drawing on the interpretative approach, which we introduced in Chapter 4.4, we will discuss here, which EQF Levels of Knowledge, Skills and Competence correspond with three competence standards for Career Advisors.

Example 1: Getting an idea of the options and challenges a client is facing

A particularly important competence of Career Advisors is their ability to "confirm the type of career-related challenge a client is facing, based on active listening to concerns and questions voiced by [the] client" (Domain of Career Counselling Competences). It corresponds with the task of Career Advisors to "get an idea of the options and challenges a client is facing" (p. 45).

Knowledge

The competence standard suggests that career advisors require knowledge about different types of career-related challenges, which people might face. Career-related challenges are often multi-faceted, and theoretical knowledge from diverse domains is of relevance to confirm the type of challenge, which a person is facing, including knowledge about psychological development, learning, the labour market, education systems, and different social systems (e.g. families or organisations). Due to this complexity and the uncertainty of any possible conclusion, career advisors definitely need an "awareness of the boundaries of [their] knowledge" (EQF Level 5), preferably a "critical understanding of [the] theories and principles" which they are applying (EQF Level 6).

Skills

The competence standard addresses the Career Advisor's need for active listening skills. Active listening implies the ability of a person to summarise what another person has said in one's own words (among others). The problems at stake when people talk about their careers are usually abstract. Therefore, the appropriate level of skills would certainly be EQF Level 5, which relates to "cognitive and practical skills required to develop creative solutions to abstract problems". Advanced skills, "required to solve complex and unpredictable problems in a specialised field of work or study" (EQF Level 6) would certainly be preferable though for this kind of practice, which explicitly deals with career-related questions (as a specialised field of work and study).

Competence

The competence standard expects Career Advisors to be able to clarify the type of challenge, which a client is facing. This means that they need to apply their knowledge about different types of career-related challenges for the sake of making a general evaluation. In doing so, they need to consider the information, which the client is sharing with them, and ask the right questions, if they are lacking important information. In doing so, they necessarily "take responsibility for managing [the] professional development of individuals" (EQF Level 6).

Example 2. Supporting clients in preparing applications

Another important competence of Career Advisors lies in their ability to "explain how to prepare applications for jobs and training opportunities (CVs, letters, interviews) to the level of general standards" (Domain of Career Education Competences, p. 56). It corresponds with the professional task of Career Advisors to "support clients in preparing applications" (p. 45).

Knowledge

This competence standard implies that Career Advisors need to know the general standards relating to applications for a broad diversity of jobs and training opportunities. Factual and theoretical knowledge about writing CVs, application letters and interviews (EQF Level 4) would be insufficient for this purpose, since applications always involve some degree of uncertainty, and there are many, partially conflicting ideas about the quality of application materials. This calls for "comprehensive, specialised, factual and theoretical knowledge" and "an awareness for the boundaries of that knowledge" (EQF Level 5). However, a "critical understanding of theories and principles" concerning applications and interviews would be preferable (EQF Level 6). It is at this "advanced" level of knowledge that a Career Advisor can understand which differences will exist between the expectations and strategies of different types of organisations, e.g. an employer seeking a technical assistant and a Master's programme seeking a promising researcher.

Skills

Obviously, this competence standard implies that Career Advisors can prepare applications of high quality themselves and are prepared to deal with a diversity of interview questions and assessment centre challenges. The challenge of supporting other people in preparing applications definitely calls for the ability of Career Advisors to "develop creative solutions to abstract problems" (EQF Level 5), since the approaches and techniques, which they apply and promote, need to be applicable for a wide range of applications. However, we are actually dealing with a pedagogical challenge here: Career Advisors need to be able to teach clients how to prepare applications to some extent. In doing so, they will need to be ready to deal with unforeseen learning challenges and complex questions. It would definitely be preferable for Career Advisors to demonstrate advanced skills for teaching and learning for them to perform the relevant tasks (EQF Level 6).

Competence

Necessarily, Career Advisors need to be ready to "review and develop [the] performance" of others (EQF Level 5), if they are expected to support people in preparing applications. Considering the fact that training of learners for the preparation of application materials typically also involves supportive activities in terms of reflection about their strengths and weaknesses, their goals and needs, qualifications at EQF Level 6 are more suitable for the development of this kind of a competence though. It is at EQF Level 6 that individuals "take responsibility for managing [the] professional development of individuals and groups".

Example 3: Making referrals to Career Professionals and other services

To offer a final example, Career Advisors are expected to be able to "judge when to make a referral to a Career Professional or to another professional service, based on [the] assessment of [their] own ability to provide the support needed by a client" (Domain of Social Systems Interventions Competences). This competence standard relates to their professional task of "making referrals to Career Professionals and other services, if advisable" (see page 45).

Knowledge

Necessarily, Career Advisors need a solid understanding of appropriate interventions for different types of career-related challenges, in order to make this kind of a judgment. Additionally, they need a good overview of the different types of professionals and services, which can deal with the relevant problems effectively. This definitely calls for "comprehensive, specialised, factual and theoretical knowledge" related to career-related challenges and appropriate interventions and "an awareness of the boundaries of that knowledge" (EQF Level 5). Again, a "critical understanding of theories and principles" (EQF Level 6) concerning appropriate interventions for career-related challenges, would be preferable though. Career Advisors need to be able to make their judgments about the necessity of referrals both quickly and with a high degree of certainty that they are making the right decision. This is where the critical application of abstract principles for the evaluation of a particular case becomes particularly important. For instance, relevant principles for referring someone to a Career Professional could relate to decision-making difficulties or conflicting interests of clients and their social contexts.

Skills

Making referrals can be a very sensitive issue, particularly in cultures, where the use of social services is viewed as a demonstration of personal weakness. Career Advisors need to be able to ask questions about the career-related challenges, which people face, in a sensitive way, in order to judge whether they are competent in offering the necessary support. If they conclude that a client should be referred, they will again need to demonstrate mature social and communicative skills to make a recommendation, which the client views as helpful. Ideally, Career Advisors will be able to draw on advanced social skills for this purpose, through which they can deal with "complex and unpredictable" behaviours of their clients effectively (EQF Level 6).

Competence

This competence standard requires Career Advisors to assess their own competence to offer the support needed by their clients. To do so, they definitely need to be able to "review [their own] performance" (EQF Level 5). However, they are actually "taking responsibility for decision-making in unpredictable work or study contexts": Their judgment could have a serious impact on the "professional development of individuals", which comes with an additional ethical responsibility (EQF Level 6).

5.2.2 Career Professionals

Nineteen competence standards are formulated for the academic training of Career Professionals (Table 1, pp. 56-57). Adding the competence standards for the academic training of Career Advisors, which are also relevant for Career Professionals, NICE has defined 28 competence standards for the academic training of Career Professionals. Considering this extensive competence profile, it is no surprise that NICE concludes that Career Professionals need to engage in a full academic training programme specialised in career guidance and counselling as an entry requirement to practice.

For the academic training and recognition of prior learning of Career Professional competences, NICE recommends full degree programmes at EQF Level 7, particularly specialised Master degrees or Postgraduate Diplomas. This implies that the duration of academic training for Career Professionals should amount to 1-2 full years of study at at Postgraduate or Master level (60-120 ECTS points). At the lowest, academic training should be offered in terms of specialised Bachelor programmes (EQF 6) of 3-4 years length (180-240 ECTS points).

Drawing on the interpretative approach, which we introduced in Chapter 4.4, we will discuss here, which EQF Levels of Knowledge, Skills and Competence correspond with two competence standards for Career Professionals.

Example 1: Supporting clients in the interpretation of complex situations

The first competence standard, which we will discuss here, expects Career Professionals to be able to "assess the meaning of complex life situations and different types of information together with clients, based on their interests, competences and other resources" (Domain of Career Counselling Competences, see pages 56-57). This competence standard corresponds with the professional task of Career Professionals to "support clients in the interpretation of complex situations" (see page 47).

Knowledge

It is relatively obvious from the competence definition that Career Professionals need theoretical knowledge from diverse fields, including psychology, educational sciences, economics, organisational sciences, management etc., to grasp the complete complexity of the life situations, which clients are facing, including their internal resources and the resources of their social environment. A "critical awareness of knowledge issues in a field and at the interface between fields" is clearly associated with EQF Level 7.

Skills

In terms of skills, Career Professionals need to be able to analyse a problem together with a client, i.e. partially taking on the client's perspective, respecting the client's interests and understanding of a situation. Additionally, they need problem-solving skills to customise the situational analysis to the concrete needs and resources of a client, using non-standard approaches, and integrating information, knowledge and analytical frameworks from different fields. Dealing with "work or study contexts that are complex, unpredictable and require new strategic approaches" and "specialised problem-solving skills required […] in order to integrate knowledge from different fields" are clearly linked to EQF Level 7. Career Professionals cannot afford to view the problems of their clients solely through the perspective of one discipline of thinking, or one single model of problem solving. They need to be aware of the possible relevance of many factors (psychological, physical, cultural, social, organisational…), and do so from a strategic perspective, which concentrates on supporting clients in finding solutions to their career-related challenges.

Competence

Through the multiple facets, the subjectivity and social embeddedness, and the lack of transparency and certainty, which characterises career development routes, strategic approaches are irreplaceable, when supporting a client in jeopardy. This implies weighing the potential outcomes of different action plans under constraints such as moving targets, information, which is incomplete, overwhelming or flawed, and approaching reality through an approach of "trial and error", which might imply testing and evaluating different alternatives over time. Therefore, supporting clients in the interpretation of their situations often goes beyond taking "responsibility for [the] professional development of individuals and groups", which is reflected at EQF Level 6. Instead, the focus of professional career counselling will often lie on a reinterpretation or reframing of "work or study contexts that are complex and unpredictable" for the purpose of devising "new strategic approaches" (EQF Level 7).

Example 2: Dealing with role and value conflicts effectively

Another competence standard expects Career Professionals to be able to "develop strategies to overcome personal role and value conflicts while working with clients from different backgrounds, in alignment with professional and ethical standards for career guidance and counselling" (Domain of Generic Professional Competences, Table 1, pp. 56-57). This competence standard relates to the task of Career Professionals to "deal with role and value conflicts effectively" (see page 47).

Knowledge

In terms of knowledge, the competence definition actively relates to roles, values, ethical and professional standards for career guidance and counselling, and the diverse backgrounds, which clients may have. This presupposes a large quantity of "highly specialised knowledge, some of which is at the forefront of knowledge" in the field of career guidance and counselling "as the basis for original thinking" (EQF Level 7). Professional and ethical standards for career guidance and counselling are multi-faceted and complex in their nature. Furthermore, there are many types of role and value conflicts, with which Career Professionals may need to cope, particularly in consideration of diverse value orientations and cultural backgrounds, which clients may have.

Skills

The role and value conflicts, which Career Professionals may need to deal with, are multifaceted and frequent in practice. For instance, a Career Professional working for a public employment service may be obliged to sanction particular behaviours of clients, which can easily conflict with the need to build a trustful counselling relationship. Similarly, Career Professionals may have to work with clients, who hold different values and worldviews than themselves, for example in relation to family planning (which certainly can become a relevant topic in relation to career development).

To deal with such situations effectively and ethically, they need a strong commitment to professional and ethical values. Beyond the relevant knowledge and values, they will require skills to make use of this knowledge for purposes of problem solving, so they can put their commitment into practice. In particular, they need skills for deliberating about moral dilemmas and conflicts of interest – not only for themselves, but also with clients, colleagues and other parties, e.g. employers. Sometimes, this will imply ethical reasoning in the sense of Kant's categorical imperative: "Act only according to that maxim whereby you can at the same time will that it should become a universal law without contradiction." (Kant 1993, p. 30). In terms of the EQF, the identification of a universal law for dealing with a particular role conflict or dilemma can be considered as the development of "new knowledge and procedures" via (EQF Level 7). The necessity of a Career Professional to command deliberative skills at this level comes with the complex and unpredictable problems, which may occur in the practice of career guidance and counselling, and which cannot all be addressed in a professional code of ethics.

Competence

Having to deal with role and value conflicts, which concern the professional development of individuals and groups, Career Professionals carry a high degree of responsibility. In many cases, they will find themselves confronted with conflicting values and expectations from the sides of their clients, their employers, larger society, law and other professionals. As Career Professionals, their primary role is to support clients in making sense of their situations and finding solutions for their career development – therefore, instead of making decisions for their clients, they will need to support their clients in deliberating about different alternatives. In consideration of their clients' diverse backgrounds, they will need a high level of empathy and intercultural competence for this purpose, so they can understand what is important for their clients. At the same time, they will need to be able to formulate conflicting organisational and/or societal expectations in such a way that clients can consider them as factors in their decision-making. Since value conflicts can become highly emotional, e.g. between a student striving for self-determination and a school's obligation to educate adolescents until a particular age, Career Professionals need to be highly self-aware and in good command of their own emotions. At the minimum, this demands for Career Professionals to "take responsibility for managing [the] professional development of individuals" (EQF Level 6). In some cases, dilemmas and conflicts will only be resolved, if Career Professional work to "manage and transform [the] work or study contexts", which are causing the relevant issues (EQF Level 7).

5.2.3 Career Specialists

The NICE Types of Career Practitioners define five general pathways for specialisation in career guidance and counselling, one for each of the NICE Professional Roles (see Chapter 3, p. 48). The underlying idea is that specialists are needed in each of these five domains, who are ready to innovate practice in these realms at a systemic level. From this point of view, the central characteristic of diverse specialist roles is that the Career Specialists' responsibility goes beyond their own professional practice in targeting innovation and development regarding how large numbers of career practitioners perform career guidance and counselling.

For the academic training and recognition of prior learning of Career Specialist competences, NICE recommends reference to EQF Level 8, e.g. as part of structured doctoral training. At the lowest, training should be provided in terms of specialised Postgraduate certificates or Master Degrees (EQF 7). We recommend a minimum of 30 ECTS points worth of academic training for Career Specialist qualifications, building on prior training as a Career Professional. This training should be part of a PhD programme (180-240 ECTS) or of a Specialised Master Degree (60-120 ECTS), which has a strong focus on competences for research and development.

Altogether, 14 competence standards have been formulated explicitly for the different types of Career Specialists (Table 1, pp. 56-57). Three competence standards have been identified as relevant for all Career Specialists, independent of the professional role(s), which they specialise on (Domain of Generic Professional Competences). They refer to tasks in academic training and research in career guidance and counselling and the promotion of this kind of specialised training and research. From the perspective of NICE, the relevant competences are of central importance for all types of Career Specialists, since they enable them to take on a larger, systemic responsibility for the development of career guidance and counselling. For example, managers of large career services need to be capable of providing high-quality training for employees, if they want to innovate the practice of career guidance and counselling in their organisations. Similarly, they will need to be able to conduct research up to scientific standards in assessing the quality and outcomes of their organisation's career services.

The relevant qualification level for the training of Career Specialists becomes most evident, when looking at particular competence standards. Many competence standards relate to the design of scientifically validated approaches, tools and instruments for the practice of career guidance and counselling and for relevant research. Drawing on the interpretative approach, which we introduced in Chapter 4.4, we will discuss here, which EQF Levels of Knowledge, Skills and Competence correspond with two of the competence standards for Career Specialists.

Example 1: Developing assessment approaches and instruments

Career Specialists in Career Assessment and Information are expected to be able to "design career assessment approaches and tools [...], to provide a relevant and reliable diagnosis of people's career related interests, abilities, competences, motivations and other characteristics." (Table 1, pp. 56-57).

Knowledge

Innovative assessment approaches and instruments used in career guidance and counselling should be based on the most advanced knowledge concerning people's interests, competences, motivations and other characteristics. Relevant knowledge will concern the latest theories on the constructs, which shall be assessed, and the knowledge of theories for scientific testing and evaluation (among others). The relevance of the approaches and instruments for the practice of career guidance and counselling, which takes place at the interface between different fields, including education and work, also demands critical knowledge about the diverse contexts, in which such approaches and instruments are used. Necessarily, Career Specialists should draw on "knowledge at the most advanced frontier of [their] field of work or study and at the interface between fields" (EQF Level 8), if the approaches and instruments, which they design, shall be of significant relevance and reliability for practice.

Skills

The underlying goal of this competence standard is clearly to "solve critical problems in research and/or innovation and to extend and redefine existing knowledge or professional practice" (EQF Level 8). Career Professionals are already expected to demonstrate the ability to "assess particular resources, interests or other relevant characteristics of an individual client using a suitable career assessment approach of high validity in a collaborative way" (Domain of Career Assessment and Information Competences). The challenge for Career Specialists in Career Assessment and Information is to innovate the approaches and instruments available for practice and research, thereby solving critical problems of existing approaches and instruments. For this purpose, they should be able to evaluate the ability of existing approaches and instruments to provide relevant information in an efficient and ethically correct way, thereby validating them and investigating their performance. For a reliable, state-of-the-art evaluation, relevant Career Specialists will need to draw on "the most advanced and specialised skills and techniques" for the scientific validation of assessment approaches and instruments.

Competence

The level of autonomy and responsibility demanded from a Career Specialist who designs assessment approaches and instruments is substantial. Above all, this work requires a high degree of self-criticality and scientific rigour: Empirical and theoretical constructs and approaches need to be validated and re-validated until their functionality has been proven up to scientific standards. Accordingly, Career Specialists should "demonstrate substantial authority, innovation, autonomy, scholarly and professional integrity" as well as "sustained commitment to the development of new ideas or processes at the forefront of work or study contexts including research" (EQF Level 8).

Example 2: Evaluating the quality of career services for their further development

Looking at a more practically oriented competence, Career Specialists in Career Service Management are expected to be able to "evaluate the quality of techniques and programme evaluation models used in career services, applying standards and expertise on innovative and effective practices." (Table 1, pp. 56-57)

Knowledge

As a framework for their evaluative activities, Career Specialists in Career Service Management are expected to refer to specific standards. Such references ensure that a systematic and professional evaluation is grounded on state-of-the art practices and the latest knowledge in the practice of evaluation. Relevant standards will certainly include quality standards for evaluation, as well as quality standards for career guidance and counselling, perhaps even for the management of career services. Clearly, the relevant knowledge needed is "highly specialised", some of it "at the forefront of knowledge" in the field of career guidance and counselling (EQF Level 7), particularly since evaluators need to be able to work with this type of knowledge at a level of critical assessment. Additionally, the Career Specialists are also expected to apply "expertise on innovative and effective practices" in their evaluative activities, however. This means that they also need to be knowledgeable about new trends and developments in the management of career services, and particularly well informed about the outcomes of research on the quality and effectiveness of career guidance and counselling. Ideally, Career Specialists in Career Service Management will therefore possess "knowledge at the most advanced frontier" on career guidance and counselling and career service management in particular, for their practice as evaluators (EQF Level 8).

Skills

The systematic evaluation of career services, which also looks at the quality of mechanisms used to collect relevant information, including information about the outcomes of the career services, targets at the innovation of career services. Clearly, the relevant Career Specialists need to be able to operationalise complex norms and quality criteria for the process of inquiry and observation. In the EQF, skills for evaluation are generally related to EQF Level 8. Synthesis and evaluation are seen among the "most advanced and specialised skills and techniques [...] required to solve critical problems in research and/or innovation and to extend and redefine existing knowledge or professional practice" (EQF Level 8). The extension and redefinition of professional practice is precisely the goal of evaluating career services for their further development. It could be argued that in regards of non-critical problems, an EQF Level 7 qualification would be sufficient. EQF Level 7 demands for "specialised problem-solving skills [...] in order to develop new knowledge and procedures and to integrate knowledge from different fields." However, resolving non-critical problems of career services is more of what should be expectable from any Career Professional. A person who professionally evaluates career services, should certainly be able to detect issues, which require a critical perspective, and develop effective solutions together with the responsible Career Professionals.

Competence

Career Specialists engaged in the evaluation of career services have a special responsibility for the development and quality assurance of career guidance and counselling in our contemporary societies. Evaluators of career services are regularly the authorities based on whose judgment a career service's quality is viewed as acceptable or inacceptable. This evaluative power must come with a high degree of autonomy and professional integrity on the one hand: Multiple interests are at stake when a career service is assessed, and an evaluation needs to be fair, truthful and reliable. Career Specialists evaluating career services therefore need to manage relationships with their clients and other interested parties in a highly professional way. On the other hand, relevant Career Specialists also need to demonstrate a "sustained commitment to the development of new ideas [and] processes at the forefront" of career guidance and counselling, if they shall contribute to the development of career services in general (EQF Level 8). In the selection of their assessment techniques and evaluation models and standards, they must be able to work with state-of-the-art practices and theories and combine them adequately to evaluate the relevant service or programme. The findings of their evaluative activities should be of such quality, transparency and practical relevance that the service providers will be able to draw reasonable conclusions for the further development of their career services. Furthermore, the results should also be useful for research around the quality management of career services. Such knowledge is also crucial for the further development of existing quality standards and legislation around the quality assurance of career services.

QUALITY ASSURANCE AND ENHANCEMENT: POLICY AND PRACTICE

by Rachel Mulvey and Roberta Piazza

The partners of the NICE network have worked collaboratively to articulate European Competence Standards in this handbook as well as common points of reference (NICE 2012). This demonstrates a shared understanding that quality benchmarks are considered to be essential for the effective training of career practitioners. Notwithstanding this intrinsic motivation, the changing external operating environment for higher education providers across Europe makes increasing demands from the quality perspective. The Bologna Declaration (1999) is pre-eminent here alongside the more commercial aspect of universities needing to demonstrate value for money to governments and students alike.

This chapter considers how programme leaders (at university level) can first assure the quality of their courses from the outset (quality assurance), and then engage in a process of continuous quality enhancement for as long as the programme is offered. The chapter identifies sources of relevant European policies along with sources of support and guidance to colleagues in the community of practice who are working through quality processes. It argues that engaging with quality assurance and enhancement (QAE) can take many forms; it can be a formal process or an informal action, an evaluative reporting process or an individual act of reflection by a career practitioner involved in training. A checklist offers an overview of what is typically included in formal evaluation of a degree programme.

The chapter goes on to discuss how the competence standards and common points of reference from NICE can be used for quality assurance and enhancement of academic training. For demonstration, NICE partners share their experience of using the competence standards and common points of reference in QAE. These illustrations are adapted from items previously published in NICE newsletters between 2013 and 2015.

6.1 Policy Drivers

For many decades, the European Union regarded education as a state-level concern, until the creation of the European Higher Education Area (EHEA) was seen as a key way of promoting the mobility and employability of all EU citizens. The Sorbonne Declaration (1998) therefore proposed that the segmentation of the higher education sector in Europe was outdated and harmful. It stressed the importance of education and educational cooperation in the development and strengthening of stable, peaceful and democratic societies and aimed to harmonise the architecture of the European Higher Education Area.

The Bologna Declaration (1999), along with the subsequent Bologna Process, consisted of a voluntary commitment of each signatory country to reform its own education system. The over-arching intention was to create "a more complete and far-reaching Europe" through "strengthening its cultural, social, scientific and technological dimensions". Far-reaching here could be understood as a reference to the increased geographical spread of the EU. The specific focus was to increase the competitiveness of the EHEA. It is important to note that this reform was not imposed on the national governments or universities. The legal was the Maastricht Treaty, which clearly permitted joint action in the field of education "while fully respecting the responsibility of the Member States for the content of teaching and the organisation of education systems and cultural and linguistic diversity" (Maastricht Treaty 1992, Article 126).

The Bologna Process has been an important driver of change and reform in European higher education, working towards a EHEA, where qualifications issued in one European country will we recognised in other European countries. A couple of major achievements are:

- The *Framework for Qualifications for the European Higher Education Area* (Bergen 2005, Appendix 1), through which the three academic cycles (Bachelor, Master and Doctorate) are becoming standardised across Europe[1], and

- The *European Credit Transfer and Accumulation System* (ECTS), promoting student-centred learning based on clearly articulated learning outcomes (ECTS Users' Guide 2015).

Quality assurance has gained a prominent role in the Bologna Process. In 2003, the ministers responsible for higher education recognised that the "quality of higher education has proven to be at the heart of the setting up of a European Higher Education Area" (Berlin 2003, p. 3). They also stressed that "the primary responsibility for quality assurance in higher education lies with each institution itself and this provides the basis for real accountability of the academic system within the national quality framework" (ibid.).

---

1 The three academic cycles are endorsed in the European Qualifications Framework for Lifelong Learning (EQF 2008).

This respect for university autonomy has been retained and is still evident in current reports (e.g. European Commission et al. 2015). As the last Report on *Progress in Quality Assurance in Higher Education* highlights, higher education institutions "have the ultimate responsibility for the quality of their offering (setting, monitoring and renewing their quality goals through ‚internal' quality assurance)" (European Commission 2014, p. 3). However, as the report goes on, they are nowadays supported by external quality assurance agencies (QAAs), which assess quality standards, evaluate institutions, accredit programmes or benchmark the performance of higher education institutions against each other (ibid.). Public authorities are seen to have a duty "to ensure that the quality of individual institutions, and of their higher education system as a whole, are fit for purpose" (ibid.). Where national QAAs offer reference points, higher education providers have a shared starting point to set, describe and assure the quality and academic standards of their degree programmes. For example, the British QAA reports on the higher education institutions they assess, outlining how the QAA's criteria are met and what recommendations for improvement have been made. Additionally, the QAA offers examples of good practice.

By quality assuring the programme of study offered, the programme leader concerned is able to ensure that academic standards, academic quality and any relevant information about their higher education provision are all comparable to other higher education institutions nationally and within Europe. In addition, effective quality assurance activities, ensuring that programmes are well-designed, monitored and periodically reviewed, help to establish and maintain the confidence of students and other stakeholders in higher education institutions. This enables students and graduates greater mobility within Europe, and helps higher education providers to ensure that graduates have the right skills for the labour market and to reduce skills mismatches.

At the European level, the *European Quality Assurance Register for Higher Education* (EQAR) has been established to help harmonise quality assurance across Europe. National QAAs, which are registered with EQAR, shall be able to perform their activities across the European Higher Education Area, i.e. in 47 countries, while complying with national requirements (Bucharest 2012, p. 2). The existence of an institution like EQAR is particularly important for the quality assurance of joint degree programmes of higher educations from different countries, and for the coordination of quality assurance systems across Europe. Furthermore, common *Standards and Guidelines for Quality Assurance in the European Higher Education Area* shall contribute to the "common understanding of quality assurance for learning and teaching across borders among all stakeholders" (ESG 2015, p. 4). Many activities like these are going on at the European level, which shall help to build mutual trust and better recognition of qualifications and programmes between countries in the future. Appendix 2 presents an overview of relevant resources.

Table 3 presents an overview of important questions for the quality assurance and enhancement of degree programmes in the form of a checklist. The exact requirements for the validation of new programmes and the enhancement of existing programmes will vary from one university to another, because each university has autonomy in its power to award degrees. Nevertheless, because of the harmonisation through the Bologna Process (1999), it is likely that most universities will consider similar issues when assuring quality. In relation to the approval, monitoring and periodic review of programmes and awards, the ENQA (2009) defines some guidelines to assure the quality of programmes.

Checklist: Quality Assurance and Enhancement of Degree Programmes	
Validity of the Assurance Process ✓ Are there formal programme approval procedures by a body other than that teaching the programme? For example, does a national quality assurance agency or an accreditation body make prescriptions?	**Academic Climate and Resources** ✓ Are there enough suitably qualified staff to teach the programme? ✓ Are there adequate resources including books, computers, teaching rooms? ✓ Are appropriate learning resources available?
Structure, Design and Curriculum Content ✓ Is the purpose and target group of the programme described in a programme profile? ✓ Are the overall aims and objectives of the programme appropriate for its purpose? ✓ Are explicit intended learning outcomes developed and published? ✓ Has careful attention been paid to curriculum design and content? ✓ Does the curriculum enable the student to meet the learning outcomes? ✓ Is the curriculum in line with similar programmes offered nationally and internationally? ✓ Are the credit points (ECTS) awarded for courses aligned to the actual workload of learners?	**Learning, Teaching and Assessment Methods** ✓ Is there a range of methods used for teaching and learning? ✓ Are the methods of teaching and learning appropriate in view of the learning outcomes defined in the curriculum? ✓ Are individual student needs taken into account in teaching? ✓ Is the assessment appropriate to assess the published learning outcomes? ✓ Is there a range of assessment methods? ✓ Are the specific needs of different modes of delivery (e.g. full time, part-time, distance learning, e-learning) and types of higher education (e.g. academic, vocational, professional) demonstrably considered? ✓ Is there monitoring of the progress and achievements of students?
Reviews and Quality Enhancement ✓ Are there regular periodic reviews of programmes? ✓ Do reviews include external panel members? ✓ Are students adequately involved in quality assurance activities? ✓ Is feedback from employers, labour market representatives and other relevant organisations sought on a regular basis?	**Information Policy** ✓ Is up to date, impartial and objective information (both quantitative and qualitative) about the programmes and awards regularly published? ✓ Are transcripts of records offered, which allow for transnational mobility and the recognition of degrees in other countries?

Table 3: Checklist: Quality Assurance and Enhancement of Degree Programmes, all rights reserved

6.2 How NICE supports Quality Assurance and Enhancement

The European Competence Standards (ECS), the NICE Professional Roles (NPRs) and the NICE Curriculum Framework are valuable resources for the organisation and benchmarking of academic training for career practitioners. They offer common points of reference, which are external to any one university, and which represents a strong pan-European consensus based on sound research activities by experts in the field. They are of particular value in combination with the formal quality assurance and enhancement mechanisms featured above, because they add a content-related dimension.

Using the ECS and common points of reference (CPRs) can strengthen the argument for recognition of proposed degree programmes. The NICE Professional Roles are helpful in delineating what students on the proposed course are being trained to deliver in terms of their professional practice on eventual graduation. The ECS relate to these roles in defining competence standards for three types of career practitioners. They are expressed in terms of performance-oriented competences, which are assessable as a clear set of learning outcomes. The ECS are a tool that can be used by higher education institutions and teaching staff to design the curriculum (and their research and teaching activities) to help the students to acquire those competences. The ECS can therefore be considered a way to implement a strategy for the continuous quality enhancement and to increase the development of a quality culture, which recognises the importance of quality, and quality assurance, in their work. The NICE Curriculum Framework articulates resource requirements in terms of cognitive (competence-specific knowledge), affective (attitudes, values, motivations) and behavioural resources (physical and cognitive skills). Together the CPR support the development of programmes of professional training which stand up to the rigour of quality assurance for initial validation and frame continual quality enhancement for the life of the programme.

The NICE network comprises experts in the field of career education, guidance and counselling who are all peers in the European community of practice. This offers a rich opportunity for professional reflection and peer review in the process of quality assurance. Formal quality assurance processes often require the input of an external expert to confirm the level and organisation of a proposed programme is at a similar level to comparable courses elsewhere. This is reflected in the checklist on quality assurance and enhancement above (Table 3).

Beyond the expectations of a formal accreditation process, the network can enrich teaching and learning through more informal processes. This could be a simple critical reading of quality documentation, or a reality-check conversation with peers in the NICE network. A more elaborate process of this kind of peer learning, a methodology tested by a number of NICE peers across national boundaries, is presented in Chapter 7.

NICE partners have made use of the common points of reference (CPRs) both for informal and formal processes of quality assurance and enhancement. Relating to the checklist (Table 3), the following illustrations demonstrate how the achievements and products of NICE can be used in practice. They have been provided by NICE members, and are based on their experience in applying the CPR in the past years.

Validity of the Assurance Process

"The common points of references from NICE (2012), especially the NICE Core Competences, the NICE Curriculum Framework and the NICE Professional Roles, were used to help develop a new 60 ECTS postgraduate programme at the University of the Faroe Islands. The NICE Curriculum Framework provided an important common benchmark and language to discuss the curriculum, in particular what to include and what to leave out. The NICE Professional Roles were used to introduce the question of professionalism to students and to explore current practices. This discussion was helpful for refining the programme and its curriculum further. Most importantly, the common points of references offer a solid foundation for the programme development and the visual presentations. The descriptions provide a good overview of issues and tools for communication and discussion with all parties."

Sif Einarsdóttir, University of Iceland

Academic Climate and Resources

"The NICE Professional Roles and the NICE Core Competences played a role in ensuring the academic climate and resources reach quality benchmarks, when guidance professors from 16 Spanish universities came together for the National Seminar of the Spanish Interuniversity Guidance Professors Network. An important conclusion of the seminar was that the NICE depiction of professional roles permits different types of guidance intervention to align, in allowing for a variation in context. The NICE Professional Roles can also be used as a bench mark against which relative strengths and weaknesses in the professional performance can be identified. This will help to project guidelines for the initial training (which must be common) and continuous formation of guidance professionals to enable their occupational performance and mobility."

Luis M. Sobrado Fernandez, University of Santiago de Compostela, Spain

Structure, Design and Curriculum Content of the Programme

"The JAMK University of Applied Sciences in Finland has already built its career guidance and counselling education curriculum around the NICE Core Competences from 2012. It was therefore a logical step to apply the new European Competence Standards (2015) to their continuing and further education offer. Modules were selected and linked to build a relatively short course, comprising 25 credits. This course is aimed at people who working in the field, that is, offering career services – but as advisors or supporters rather than as certified career professionals. Validating a credit-rated short course means that in the future, if a person applies to JAMK for a full length career guidance and counselling education programme, their advisor-level studies will be acknowledged as having been formally accredited, which speeds up progress through the course."

Seija Koskela, Jyväskylä University of Applied Sciences (JAMK), Finland

"The Postgraduate certificate Expert in Job Placement Services, funded through the European Social Fund, opened to 18 participants, was redesigned in its second edition, using the CPRs. The competences were used to re-adapt the teaching modules, the teaching methodologies and the assessment practices. Currently, the course is the only one of its type in Italy. Many Postgraduate courses in guidance exist, but not in the specific sector of job placement. Considering the uniqueness of the course in the Italian scenario, the comparison with international guidelines to define the competences the professionals should have, has helped the course to acquire a broader perspective. The most important shift has been to change the overall aim from training an expert in job placement to a professional practitioner with more competences in career guidance activities."

Roberta Piazza, University of Catania, Italy

"The first Master level programme in Coaching Psychology in the Netherlands was validated at the Work and Organisational Psychology Department of the University of Amsterdam. Successful students demonstrate they have developed competences in line with the competence level promoted by NICE, including EQF level 6 competences of career advisors and EQF level 7 competences required from career professionals. The crosscutting areas of competence were derived from the NICE Professional Roles, specifically in the areas of career counselling, career service management, social systems interventions and generic professional functions."

Tim Theeboom, Annelies E.M. Van Vianen and Bianca Beersma,

University of Amsterdam, Netherlands

Learning, Teaching and Assessment Methods

"The NICE competence standards have been used in relation to quality assurance, not only for revisiting curriculum content, but also as a framework for reflective practice. Whilst the majority of the students at Aarhus Diploma Programme in Educational and Vocational guidance are career guidance counsellors, teachers were also very interested in the reach of the NICE competence standards, and the material included in the Common Points of Reference. The CPRs were used to frame discussions to consider whether the curriculum does translate in practice through activities such as planning, implementation and evaluation of teaching. Thus, the NICE material is helpful for the students at the Diploma Programme in order to contribute to an overall perspective on their own practice and on how the guidance tasks are organized in their own employing organisation. This dual process, of analysing both one's own practice and that of one's organisation contributes to strengthening the identity of the professionals involved, by developing aspects of the role of the career counsellor within a clear framework."

Rita Buhl and Randi Boelskifte, VIA University College, Denmark

"Formal evaluation from students on the MSc Career Coaching showed that they had found some parts of a lecture on career theory a bit confusing. Alerted to this block to learning, the programme leader was determined to try something new. Research on relevant theories of learning brought her to the presentations-by-students teaching method. Students in small groups (2-3 students) are assigned to different aspects of the course that they attend. They have to prepare a brief presentation (using PowerPoint or other material) regarding their assigned subject. They present this to their fellow students as a teaching session. In doing so, the whole group adopts the role of peer teacher. In order to do that, they have to read and compare several peer reviewed international and/or national journal articles. Then, the issues are discussed, and students exchange opinions regarding the strengths and weaknesses of each theory; and they examine their practical implications in different situations. Both student satisfaction and student performance increased, albeit on a small sample."

Julia Yates, University of East London, United Kingdom

Reviews and Quality Enhancement

"The Danube University Krems revalidated its post-graduate study programmes in career guidance and counselling, which cover: the development of career counselling; career education; career assessment & information competences, alongside management competences and generic professional competences. The updated curricula are already based on the European

Competence Standards of NICE. In conducting the revision of the curricula, Krems colleagues experienced the competence standards as a very helpful reference tool, which provided orientation for the developmental work of the revalidation process."

Monika Petermandl, Danube University Krems, Austria

"We used the NICE Core Competences (2012) to redesign our course contents, particularly those relating to professionalism, career education, career counselling and ethics. A team of internal and external experts undertook our review and we were delighted that Sif Einarsdóttir, our Icelandic partner, was able to join us as an external colleague. Sif made a significant contribution to the discussion and helped us to demonstrate that we are promoting 'internationalisation' and 'innovation in teaching and learning' by working with and supporting our students."

Graham Allan and Janet Moffett,

University of the West of Scotland, United Kingdom

"In the last couple of years, as a direct result of the Bologna Process, there has been university-wide activity around harmonising our existing quality processes including a taskforce, which collects and analyses data on student achievement, which in turn informs quality enhancement. We've re-organised and standardised the module handbooks and have used the NICE descriptors as a kind of benchmark in this process. We have seen this as a chance to reflect, and to sharpen our focus. The NICE Professional Roles have helped to frame student destinations and to reflect greater sensitivity around the different professional roles our students will be taking up once qualified. It has helped us ensure that our study programme prepares students for their professional practice."

Peter Weber, University of Heidelberg, Germany

7

PEER LEARNING FOR THE QUALITY ENHANCEMENT OF DEGREE PROGRAMMES

by Sif Einarsdóttir, Lucy Hearne, Margit Rammo, Peter Weber and Frida Wikstrand

The European Competence Standards are the major results presented in this publication. Another important goal was to make use of the common points of reference (CPRs) published as results from the first period of NICE (2012). NICE has started a process where groups of partners employ the CPRs and the new standards to develop their own programmes. The cooperation in the NICE network has also fostered the development of another important but less tangible resource: a community of practice for the design and implementation of degree programmes in different countries and contexts with many ties and a cooperative culture (Petermandl 2014). The NICE network provides a fertile ground for the sharing of practices, expertise and experiences. To make the most of the knowledge and social resources of the network's members, a framework for a supportive and constructive collaboration or peer learning was developed.

Peer learning (Topping 2005) is the concept that best captures the sharing of practice and experiences that are needed to facilitate the implementation of the European Competence Standards and CPRs in career guidance and counselling (CGC) programmes across Europe. Peer learning refers to strategies that involve learning through other learners (Topping 2001). In the context of study programmes in CGC, it refers to planned workshops or meetings (or series of workshops and meetings) for the improvement of a study programme in a collegial way. In this chapter, the use and value of peer learning for quality enhancement and increased cooperation between CGC programmes is discussed. Theoretical foundations are introduced and three specific peer-learning activities with a number of NICE members are described. Case studies on these activities were used to develop guidelines for peer learning. In the following sections, the case study methodology and three PL activities are described along with the moderation process. Finally, the guidelines for peer learning are presented as well as reflections on the challenges encountered by the NICE members in the practice of peer learning.

7.1 Peer Learning in the Context of Academic Training

Study programmes and staff capacity can be developed through the exchange of perspectives, co-mentoring and collegial counselling techniques like peer learning. Different terms have been used to discuss such exchanges, as well as diverse theoretical approaches, which are presented here in the context of quality enhancement. Most importantly, peer learning is seen as complementary to formal quality procedures, and provides opportunity for the empowerment of academics in CGC programmes. Therefore, we use the broader and less formal term quality enhancement instead of quality assurance.

7.1.1 Peer Learning as a Method for Quality Enhancement

Peer learning for quality enhancement in the context of NICE refers to the theory and practice of diverse forms of teamwork and collegial collaboration of CGC academics across institutions and countries. The process of this type of collegial support can be approached from many theoretical and practical points of view. For example, different perspectives focus on organisational development and quality enhancement (Schiersmann & Thiel 2014; Weber 2013), collegial counselling or peer-group supervision (e.g. Tietse 2013; Borders 1991) and educational peer learning (e.g. Topping, 2005).

In the academic training context, Topping's definition of **peer learning** appears most appropriate: "Peer learning can be defined as the acquisition of knowledge and skills through active helping and supporting among status equals or matched companions" (Topping 2005, p. 631). Topping (2005) proposes that peer learning is not restricted to intra-institutional activities, but that it can also be conducted inter-institutionally, i.e. between different educational institutions. Thus, the peer-learning approach offers NICE a blueprint for informal and participant-driven formats of mutual exchanges of expertise and experiences amongst colleagues from different study programmes. It builds upon our collective practice of coming together in the network and sharing how we set up, maintain and develop our degree programmes. It allows colleagues to describe and reflect on their own practice in terms of developing and delivering study programmes. Through listening and discussion, all participants in peer-learning activities have the opportunity to learn more about their peers' professional practice as well as their own, which is often based on more implicit than explicit knowledge until participants start to describe it to others.

As described, NICE endorses peer learning as an approach to improve the quality of study programmes in the field of CGC. Peer learning in this sense has a long tradition in the CGC field. For instance, since the 1990's many study programmes have cooperated in establishing and enhancing study programmes in Central and Eastern Europe including in Latvia, Poland, and the Slovak Republic. In the last few years, the VALA Nordplus network has been another very informative and promising example.[1] In addition, the CEDEFOP approach to developing a competence framework for the training of career practitioners can be seen in this tradition (CEDEFOP 2009). In NICE we try to formalise peer learning by capturing its essence and developing practical guidelines. Documented peer-learning experiences will help NICE partners to learn about how study programmes can make use of the common points of reference (CPRs) and competence standards (ECS) of NICE, to discover problems and obstacles. The knowledge gained from testing and validating the different tools in the practice of degree-programme development can also be instructive to work on the tools themselves in the future and refine them with more knowledge coming directly from practice.

Peer learning in this tradition of improving study programmes is an alternative to other quality approaches (see Chapter 6). Formally, quality assurance in higher education is usually ensured through national and institutional policies, requiring measures such as accreditation, evaluation or quality management. Solely implementing quality management models or quality assurance tools is a practice, which often leads to non-intended side effects. A recent study shows how educators often have to implement complicated quality regulations, which are ignored by staff, or which are very inefficient, reducing the time available for good practice in teaching and the direct contact with the students (Weber 2013, p. 164). This suggests that developmental and learning approaches should be adopted to complement more formal quality assurance models. Peer learning intends to stimulate the reflection of relevant individuals on the need for change and possibilities for further development of their own practice. Developmental approaches shift the focus away from external pressure and emphasise that goals for change should come from the inner logic of the study programme and relevant staff. The people involved need to be in charge and feel responsible when it comes to the quality of their work. The enhancement of degree programmes should be conceived as a self-organised process (Weber 2015).

7.1.2 Five Principles for Quality Enhancement through Peer Learning

Both in theory and practice, change processes deal with complex, non-predictable developments. The crucial question is how such processes can be stimulated for the empowerment of individuals and the improvement of social systems. Five basic principles are outlined here, which help to characterise peer learning as a process of change where the participants take responsibility for the process. They combine basic assumptions about how to stimulate quality enhancement (Weber 2015) and how to organise peer learning (Topping 2005) within and across organisations.

---

1 VALA is a network of career counselling and guidance programmes at higher education institutions in the Nordic and Baltic countries. Eighteen partner institutions have joined hands and established a network to be able to better prepare career counsellors and guidance workers for the diverse clients they need to work with. http://www.peda.net/en/portal/vala.

First, the key to mutual exchange of expertise and experiences is the establishment of a **stable working alliance.** Learning and change should not only be understood as an intrapersonal and cognitive process, but also as an interactional process between individuals. Thus, the interplay of people within the learning setting (e.g. an organisation, a study programme, a network) is highly relevant. The importance of building relationships and trust between a moderator or consultant and the involved people in an organisation or between the actors within an organisation or network cannot be overstated. A good relationship is an important premise for people to collaborate in a positive and constructive way.

Second, it is important to understand and organise peer learning as an **intentional learning process**. Intentionality is a relevant prerequisite for learning in general. When we think of learning not only as individual learning that occurs "all the time", but also as an organised event, we start to operationalise learning goals and form a shared intention for the learning process. In the context of NICE, we have formulated, for example, the collective goal of reaching common competence standards through our study programmes.

Third, **time and space for reflection** need to be factored into the process. Reflection is a core impetus for change processes in all kinds of human systems. In moving from the procedural level (how to organise peer learning) to a deeper process of change and development, we must regard reflection as very important practice (Reid & Bassot 2012, p. 180). The course of intentional (quality) development within a good working alliance is energised by reflective practices.

The first three first principles refer to the learning processes. However, we also need to pay attention to the context. The fourth principle relates to the importance of understanding the institutional context of change by **analysing the current situation and focusing on the change process**. Peer-learning events are aimed at triggering change processes in organisations. For strategic reasons, planned change should be based on an analysis of the current situation, for example of an organisation or a study programme. This is necessary, because to stimulate change, one needs to have an idea about things as they are right now. Change processes also need a clear focus, so we know which aspects to concentrate on in peer learning and which to ignore for the moment.

Finally, change processes face environmental boundaries, so the fifth principle addresses the need to **make environmental boundaries visible and work towards change**. For example, an intended organisational change may be restricted by the available resources, norms, rules and regulations, or the disciplinary tradition of an existing study programme. Particularly where goals of learning in organisations usually follow the normative logic of the organisation, mutual learning approaches can help to discover and understand existing constraints. Together, partners can identify possibilities of change (e.g. by formulating goals) and possibly even overcome some constraints, which one single partner could not have resolved alone.

7.2 Peer Learning in Practice: Three Case Studies

The European Competence Standards (ECS) and the common points of reference (CPRs) of NICE have been used in various ways to develop quality programmes. The NICE Core Competences (NICE 2012) and the ECS have been used most often, but the NICE Curriculum Framework and the NICE Professional Roles have also been applied in various ways (see Chapter 6). NICE network members came together for three different peer-learning activities during the period from May 2014 to May 2015: in Gödöllö, Hungary, in Bordeaux, France, and in Mannheim, Germany. The aim of the activities was to either establish a new degree programme in career guidance and counselling or to develop aspects of existing programmes through the sharing of ideas and good practices amongst the members of the specific peer-learning group.

A descriptive case study methodology was used to capture and document the particular type of collaboration. Case studies provide a "unique example of real people in real situations" (Cohen et al. 2011, p. 289) and are used for a number of reasons in education, guidance counselling and therapeutic research (Hearne 2011; McLeod 2015; Yin 2009). Generally, case studies are the chosen method when "(a) 'how' or 'why' questions are being posed; (b) the investigator has little control over events; and (c) the focus in on a contemporary phenomenon within a real-life context" (Yin 2009, p. 2). In the different case studies, participant observation was used: Members of the peer-learning group not only observed and recorded the work, but also engaged collegially in the activity with the other participants (Cohen et al. 2011). The following two sections will discuss the moderation of the peer-learning activities, and present the three different case studies in the form of case vignettes.

7.2.1 Moderation of Peer Learning Activities

As discussed already, peer learning is a concrete approach to stimulate learning and organisational change (at least when it refers to the development of study programmes). Its success relies on realising the five principles presented above. Therefore, we have decided to work with a model, which characterises problem solving as a cyclical process (see Figure 8). Within a peer-learning activity, the eight phases of this problem-solving process model can be used as a procedure for improving a study programme while drawing on the ECS or CPRs. The model draws on a broad empirical basis and is very generic in its logic (Schiersmann & Thiel 2014, p. 69). It helps to organise planned learning and change processes in practice. For instance, a moderator can use it to navigate a group through a peer-learning process. The model can also be used as a tool to reflect on what has already has been reached, and to determine the next steps, which a team should work on.

The problem-solving process model is neither static nor should it be understood as a path that has to be followed exactly in the direction depicted here. It was utilised by the peer-learning groups as a heuristic with a good empirical foundation both in the problem-solving theory and in the practice of organisational change (Weber & Katsarov 2013, p. 65). The problem-solving process model indicates that complex developmental processes follow generic stages of problem solving, which are described in eight phases. By focusing on these elements and realising them, the change process will be supported in its capacity to address a problem or challenge. The applicability of the problem-solving process model in the context of NICE was tested in the peer-learning events and evaluated through the three case studies. Its phases have been integrated into the guidelines for peer learning, which are presented in Chapter 7.3.

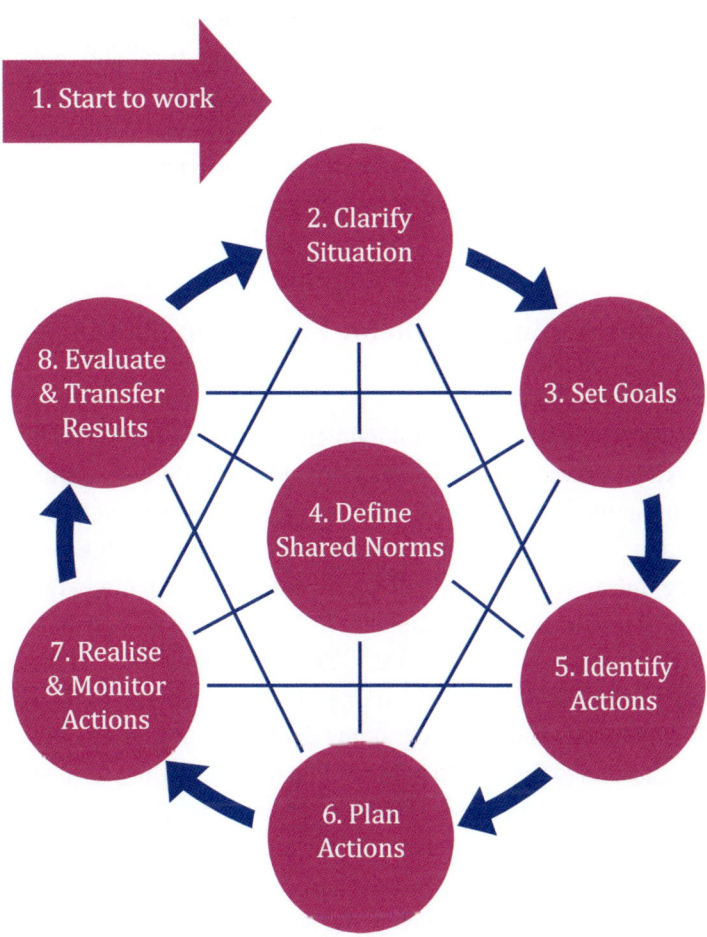

Figure 8: Problem-solving process model, adapted and translated with kind permission from C. Schiersmann & H.-U. Thiel (2014)

7.2.2 Description of Three Peer-Learning Activities

The first peer-learning event occurred in May 2014 in Gödöllö, Hungary. The second took place in Bordeaux (France) and the third in Mannheim, Germany (Spring 2015). Two members of the Peer-Learning Group also participated in a further peer-learning event in Oslo (May 2014), which is not included as a case study in this section. The three activities described here were all initiated by the Peer-Learning Group. A call was made to all NICE members to participate in peer learning for programme enhancement for the given period of time. When partners came forward with an identifiable need for development of a specific programme, interested partners were solicited for participation from within NICE. This was done both formally and in a targeted way, and informally using available communication channels (Basecamp, e-mail, conferences, working group meetings). In all three cases, the parties were interested in using the CPRs and the work focused on creating a new programme (Gödöllö), making changes to existing programmes (Bordeaux), or broadly comparing approaches in the education of career practitioners at the Bachelor level (Mannheim). The partners who had identified a need for quality enhancement usually acted as the host and invited the partners who had expressed an interest in participating. Each event lasted between two and two and a half working days and included a social and cultural activity.

Case Vignette 1: Developing a Bachelor Programme in CGC, the Case of Hungary

The first peer-learning event took place in Gödöllö, Hungary, May 2014. Two higher education institutions, Ssent István University and Eötvös Loránd University, were planning to re-establish Bachelor-level programmes in Career Guidance and Counselling. The aim was to exchange programme development experiences with participants from the NICE network. Partners from the Heidelberg University (DE), the University of Iceland (IS), the Latvian University of Agriculture (LV), Lillehammer University College (NO) and the University of Ljubljana (SI) attended the meeting and moderated the process. The event began with introductions of the different participants and their degree programmes. It then moved on to the sharing of experience about local situations, issues in programme development and the use of the CPRs. In particular, the group discussed the relation of the CPRs of NICE to the European Qualifications Framework (EQF 2008), the professional identity of career practitioners, career management competences and important knowledge areas of teaching. In the evaluation of the event, all members considered it had been useful. However, everyone also agreed that more time was needed for a deeper discussion of the topics. Trust started to emerge and developed further through social and cultural events that took place after the formal meeting. Interest in further collaboration was expressed as well as the need for a wider participation of partners, particularly those with specific experience and knowledge in developing and implementing Bachelor-level programmes in the field.

Case Vignette 2: Internationalization of a Degree Programme, the Case of Bordeaux

In April 2015 a peer-learning activity took place at the University of Bordeaux (FR). Two members of the Peer-Learning Group, from the University of Limerick (IE) and the Heidelberg University (DE), facilitated and recorded the meeting. NICE partners from the University of Iceland (IS), the University of Jyväskylä (FI) and Lillehammer University College (NO) attended. The goal of the event was to examine the possibility of broadening the University of Bordeaux's Master programme through the addition of modules or topics on ICT, Social Justice and Entrepreneurship in collaboration with the external CGC programme providers who were involved in the meeting. This new undertaking is part of an internationalisation agenda being adopted at the University of Bordeaux. Over the course of the two days, the participants shared knowledge, experience and ideas on possible ways of collaborating to develop new modules, which could be delivered via the MA programme or as part of continuing education for qualified practitioners. The NICE Core Competences (NICE 2012) were used to frame the need for curricular development and the discussion. In addition, some of the institutional issues that need to be addressed by the different members were identified, such as module design, ownership, hosting of modules through different providers, ECTS transfer, the registration of modules and travel funding for teachers and students. Additional collaboration by those in attendance was discussed with possible options put forward that included further discussions at the NICE Conference in Bratislava, May 2015. At the end of the two days, the peer-learning activity was evaluated by the two moderators for the purpose of reflecting and improving the peer-learning methodology.

Case Vignette 3: Comparing BA Programmes in Europe, the Case of Mannheim

The third peer-learning event took place in Mannheim, Germany, in May 2015. The initiative for the event came from the Gödöllö University (Hungary), based on the positive experience of the previous peer-learning activity in Hungary (see case vignette 1). The aim of this activity was to share and compare information about the different BA programmes in Europe, and to discuss future challenges for this kind of career counselling education within the NICE network. The University of Applied Labour Sciences in Mannheim hosted the event. Partners from the Gödöllö University (HU), the Heidelberg University (DE), the Jagiellonian University Krakow (PL), and the Malmö University (SE) joined. The participants presented themselves and their programmes, followed by a discussion of the different conditions provided for a BA programme in career counselling nationally. Most importantly, the group had a brainstorming discussion about future challenges for Bachelor programmes in Europe and a dialogue about future collaborations between BA programmes. The European Competence Standards were used as a reference in the discussion. The various challenges appeared to be similar between the countries. In the evaluation of the peer-learning activity, the members expressed that they had learned something new that they could use in their own settings. The group also collected different actions taken in the programme to address some of the challenges. Interest in further collaboration was articulated and the decision was made to arrange a discussion at the NICE Conference in Bratislava in May 2015, and to explore the possibility of starting a network of BA programmes in Europe.

7.3 Guidelines for Peer Learning

The lessons learned from the case studies were used to construct a framework for carrying out and moderating peer-learning activities in the context of academic training in career guidance and counselling (CGC). The elements of the framework emerged gradually. We translated them into more concrete guidelines, which can be used when applying the peer-learning strategy for quality enhancement. The guidelines also draw on our experience in working with the problem-solving process model (Figure 8). Although the use of communication technology (ICT) plays an important part in peer learning, this framework focuses mainly on the part of the peer-learning process that takes place when colleagues come together in one location to discuss programme development. Table 4 offers an overview of the three-stage framework of guidelines for peer learning, which we present in detail below.

Stage 1: Preparation

Identifying and agreeing on the aim and objectives of the peer-learning activity

The initiative for peer learning often comes from a specific degree programme or a group of colleagues facing similar needs for development in their programmes. In the case of peer learning, the process of forming an intention for the activity concerns the goals of the joint work of the involved partners. The purpose or goal of peer learning needs to be stated at least broadly at this stage (e.g. information sharing, collaboration on training or research initiatives, professional discussions). It is also important to envisage the intended outcomes of the peer-learning activity (e.g. changes for the programme, a new module, a development project). Agreeing on joint goals, relevant contents and working methodologies is an important part of the working process and demands sufficient time and awareness both before and within a meeting (intentional learning process). The peer-learning process starts right in the beginning and is at least informally moderated at this stage by the people who instigate the process and call for partners. This process corresponds with the first phase of the problem-solving process model: Start to Work (Figure 8).

Stage 1. Preparation	Stage 2. Implementation	Stage 3. Follow-Up
Identifying and agreeing on the aim and objectives of the peer-learning activity ✓ Purpose or goal stated broadly ✓ Envisage the intended outcomes **Selection of peer-learning activity partners** ✓ Find information on partners ✓ Decide whom to involve ✓ Invite partners **Deciding location, time and type of activity** ✓ Decide on type of peer learning activity ✓ Decide how and when ✓ Locate resources **Sharing of material, documents and relevant information** ✓ Share written material and on-line information	**Building trust and collaborative relationships** ✓ Discuss shared norms ✓ Share experiences, institutional context and education ✓ Create social/cultural events **Moderation** ✓ Select a moderator ✓ Introduce and apply the problem-solving process-model ✓ Keep records **Refining common goals and objectives** ✓ Discuss and construct common goals and objectives **Identify and plan action** ✓ Plan measure to reach common goals **Deciding next steps (short and long-term outcomes)** ✓ Identify short term outcomes ✓ Identify long-term outcomes ✓ Discuss how to enact the desired change	**Evaluating the outcomes of the activity for members in the group** ✓ Evaluate short term outcomes ✓ Evaluate long-term outcomes ✓ Evaluate the peer-learning process **Follow-up on the peer-learning activity after the event** ✓ Share information about the implementation activities ✓ Decide new cycle of peer learning ✓ Consider change or stability in partnership

Table 4. Guidelines for Peer Learning, all rights reserved

Selection of peer-learning activity partners

A decision needs to be made about whom to involve in the peer-learning activity from one's own institution and whom to solicit from outside (e.g. representatives of degree programmes in CGC, programme directors, lecturers, researchers, students). The former is influenced by the institutional structure, tasks and interests of different faculty members, and the relation of the work to formal quality procedures. The latter is more open but requires the use of knowledge and social ties built through the NICE network and other professional organisations. The selection of partners can be based on multiple dimensions, for example experience with the relevant task, having model of excellence, the availability of expert knowledge or having the same need for development. Similarity or difference in programme structures and content, academic affiliation, social contexts and cultures may also be taken into account. The pros and cons of creating a more homogenous or heterogeneous peer-learning group needs to be weighed. While homogeneity makes it easier to establish a stable working alliance, the diversity of perspectives in a heterogeneous group can enrich the analysis of the current situation and bring about more ideas.

Deciding location, time and type of activity

The initiators also need to decide what type of activity is suitable for the specific purpose identified by the group involved (e.g. a meeting, conference, workshop, or study visit). The question, how and where the activity shall take place (e.g. location, timing, language considerations, resourcing of travel costs), needs to be resolved based on the resources available (time and financial support). Although peer learning could occur exclusively over the internet, meeting in person and taking time to plunge into the process is recommended, because it is crucial for the creation of a stable working alliance.

Sharing of material, documents and relevant information

Sharing of written documentation relating to the goal and content of the activity (e.g. descriptions of programme, its social and institutional context, relevant career services, and quality reports) is helpful for all partners. This involves sharing of information and background of all partners, traditions in the training of career practitioners, casting light on the current situation, as well as information about institutional factors, opportunities and challenges. In the problem-solving process model (Figure 8), the sharing of material is part of Phase 2: Clarify the Situation. The written material helps the participants to get a better sense of the influencing factors that drive change or that restrict current practice. For instance, what is important in CGC practice in the relevant country, or changes regarding the organisation structures of the degree programme.

Stage 2: Implementation

Building trust and collaborative relationships

Building trust is of utter importance because it creates a collaborative atmosphere which allows for reflection – an activity, which is at the core of developmental processes as outlined above. Building trust is also supported through the problem-solving process model's fourth phase: Sharing of Norms (Figure 8). The centrality of establishing shared norms is emphasised through its location in the middle of the cycle. It is of great importance in the beginning of the peer-learning activity that the participants (probably from different higher education systems, disciplines, cultures and contexts) reflect on the shared norms underlying the peer learning they want to realise together. Some inspiration may come from cooperation in the NICE network. Talking about norms also helps to promote reflection early in the process. It can be done by building on previous relations, partnerships and by expressing the value of sharing expertise and experiences, for example. Taking time for all participants to introduce themselves (educational background, experiences and interest and role in the current activity), and the programmes they come from (disciplinary affiliation, institutional and social context) is recommended. Building social and cultural events into the process was also found to be helpful. This was often the role of the partner hosting; initiating such an event is moderating the joint undertaking, albeit by informal means.

Moderation

The selection of a formal moderator is recommended to take place at this stage. Furthermore, we propose to introduce the problem-solving process model (Figure 8) at this point in time to conceptualise and monitor the process for the participants. Moderation in this context has a variety of functions: in particular, a moderator can ensure some stability and clarity in the process and facilitate the discussions for the identification of the aims and outcomes for peer learning. Thus, the moderator takes charge of guarding and realising the five principles described above. In addition, keeping records of the activity's main outcomes (goals, discussion points, actions plans etc.) is recommended – ideally in such a way that the whole group keeps an overview. This fosters a common understanding of the major points and promotes the continuation of the process in the future. It can be helpful to elect another person for this additional role (documentation).

Refining common goals and objectives

In many cases, the team that initiates a peer-learning activity defines goals and objectives for the envisaged change process. As stated in the third phase of the problem-solving process model, Set Goals (Figure 8), goals and objectives need be discussed at the beginning of peer learning. Although they have been tentatively discussed in the preparation process, they need to be addressed more thoroughly at this stage. This is important to realise an intentional learning process, since the content, goals and expected outcomes need to be defined and agreed upon jointly. The goals and objectives direct the work of the group and influence the moderation process. Facing complexity, goals and objectives may change, which is one reason why they should be reviewed eventually as part of the process. This may help to refocus the discussion on the most relevant aspects, based on the analysis of the current situation. Although partners share common general goals they agree to work on, each partner may bring in specific needs for the development of their home programme or professional development. This is important to discuss thoroughly to ensure the mutuality of the learning process.

Identify and plan action

One of the most concrete tasks is the planning of measures to reach the identified goals and objectives (Identify Actions and Plan the Actions in the problem-solving process model; phases 5-6). This can imply joint work on the development of new teaching/learning designs or new modules, for instance. On the other hand, the participants could decide that each of them will present what they have developed at home to realise the goals they have and invite colleagues to reflect on and relate to their experience and knowledge. Planning action often deals with restrictions and constraints (make environmental boundaries visible and work toward change). Hence, thinking about possible actions is also about overcoming such restrictions, at least in a first step. In a subsequent phase, the planning of defined actions can be in focus.

Deciding next steps (short and long-term outcomes)

Short-term outcomes are often easily identified in view of the goals and objectives, which have already been specified during peer learning. Long-term outcomes may be harder to articulate. This is especially the case, when the aim is to develop a feature of a specific programme and partners are invited for consultation and collaboration. This may be easier to identify when there are common identifiable needs that different institutions work on simultaneously. The realisation of the planned actions is often the most crucial phase in change processes (Realise & Monitor the Actions as the seventh phase of the problem-solving process model). Often, this only occurs once the participants have returned to their own institutions, because peer learning has primarily focused on earlier phases of the problem-solving process model. In some cases, where colleagues from different programmes collaborate directly in the implementation (e.g. by developing mutual modules or by teacher mobility) this phase can be peer learning at its best. Working together in practice and sharing experience is a deeper way of forging alliances than the prior steps. The mutuality of the learning may help identify long-term outcomes such as intensifying the collaboration (e.g., setting up a network of BA programmes, as was the case in Mannheim).

Stage 3: Evaluation, Reflection and Follow-up

Evaluating the outcomes of the activity for members in the group

There are three types of outcomes from peer learning that can be subject to evaluations. Firstly, the concrete outcomes as expressed by the common goals, objectives and concrete actions suggested. This fits concretely with the last phase of the problem-solving process model, Evaluation & Transfer of Results, although the implementation of outcomes often rests is in the hands of the individual partners and takes place after the event. Secondly, the professional development that has taken place at the institutional and individual level. Thirdly, the peer-learning process itself, i.e. has it been helpful in building a useful collaborative relationship? Joint reflection of expectations, goals and results was applied in the three case studies and was found to be an important and a beneficial element of a mutual learning activity. In particular, it helped to build a collaborative culture and shared norms as is stated. Organising time and space for reflection for such discussions is therefore very helpful in this way. In the logic of the Organisation Development (OD) tradition, such reflection focuses on the deeper changes that occurred during a process of learning in a team or group.

Follow-up on the peer-learning activity after the event

The follow-up of the peer-learning activity should address the short-term and long-term outcomes that have been defined: How is their implementation advancing? How could it be supported further? Are there any unforeseen obstacles or opportunities, which may be addressed? Most importantly, information about the local implementation of actions should be shared with all colleagues. As in the preparation stage, the use of communication technology plays a crucial role in maintaining the collaboration for follow-up. Following up is also about maintaining a good working alliance for the future. In can also include a new cycle of peer learning, perhaps under the inclusion of further partners, as happened in the case of the meeting in Gödöllö (Hungary), after which a follow-up meeting took place in Mannheim (Germany). The sustainability and changes in the collaboration necessarily depend on the goals, outcomes and resources available.

7.4 Opportunities and Challenges of Peer Learning

The three case studies indicate that the use of peer learning for the quality enhancement of the degree programmes in Europe is a viable, useful and valued approach for NICE partners and the professionalization of career guidance and counselling (CGC). As the case vignettes and the illustrations from Chapter 6 demonstrate, there is a willingness to apply the common points of reference (CPR). Peer learning provides an opportunity to use the resources and network created through NICE to work on programme development. Nonetheless, the use of a peer-learning approach for quality enhancement in the context of academic training also has specific challenges in terms of practical application. This is partly due to the diverse social and institutional contexts of academic training in CGC across Europe. The issues that are referred to in this section relate mainly to practical problems, channels and resources for networking, the diversity of the programmes, culture and language that arose in the peer-learning activities. The lessons learned from the case studies are discussed to raise awareness of some of the challenges that may face NICE partners in using peer learning.

The first practical matter that needs to be resolved in order to conduct peer learning is the **identification and contacting of possible peer-learning partners**. The professional ties formed in the NICE network are helpful for the selection of partners, but not sufficient on their own. The continuation and sustainability of the NICE network plays a key role as a supportive structure for conducting peer-learning activities in the future. Information about possible partners needs to be available to form peer-learning groups based on structure and content of relevant study programmes, and the expertise and experience of individual academics. The NICE legacy of an online database within its website is useful here. Information about resources for mobility is also available at local universities through schemes such as ErasmusPlus or Nordplus.

Secondly, on a related practical note, the **availability of time, space and the use of online technology** needs to be considered. The guidelines for peer learning are intended for activities that take place in a physical meeting. This was the major focus of the three case studies presented here. The use of ICT should be factored into the process also, as has been pointed out, to create longer timelines of structured cooperation. Online channels and resources can be used to find information on experience and expertise of possible partners to establish contact, exchange materials and share ideas about the goals in the preparation process. The use of ICT is vital also for the follow-up and sustainability of the collaboration. Constructive use of technology for sustainable collaboration needs to be further explored and evaluated in the context of peer learning for the quality enhancement of degree programmes in CGC.

Thirdly, for peer learning to be successful, **trust and collaboration as equals** is crucial. The inter-organisational and interpersonal factors make up the informal accountability in networks (Romsek et al. 2012). The NICE Quality Group explicitly evaluated the quality of collaboration in NICE, including its circumstances (Petermandl 2014; et al. 2014). The results indicate that the communication is dynamic and a culture of mutual respect and trust has been formed. Trust and willingness to communicate and reflect freely is a key ingredient of any fruitful cooperation and needs to fostered and openly discussed in the process. Topping's (2005) approach to peer learning was selected as a framework for the case studies partly because it emphasises that the learning takes place amongst status equals. This is a key issue because we are suggesting the use of peer learning among academics running degree programmes in career guidance and counselling. However, it is likely that a programme may start a peer-learning event because of a specific need and invite colleagues to the event based on their experiences. This may create some kind of "inequality" in terms of experience and possibly expertise amongst the partners. In some cases, people may decide to form a peer-learning group with partners who are at the same stage of development and this may not be a concern. The process of sharing your own practices, experiences and expertise is always in itself a learning experience for those coming in with established knowledge. However, it may be important to counteract the possible hampering effects of inequalities, for example by having all involved partners offer their "expertise" and using the event to share practices and experiences beyond the ones in the focus of the hosts, who are organising the event. This is one way to help foster a culture of mutuality, equality and trust and solicit peer-learning partners.

Finally, **diversity and language** are major challenges facing peer-learning groups. The acknowledgement of diverse cultures, traditions, histories, contexts and disciplinary affiliations of CGC degree programmes in Europe is of absolute importance. Most programmes were established in the last 20 years, but others have been in existence for much longer. The programmes in the NICE network tend to be multidisciplinary in their nature. The majority are situated in departments of education and psychology, but some are also affiliated to sociology or business (Ertelt et al. 2012). Half of the faculty members have completed MA degrees and the other half PhDs, but few specifically in CGC (Einarsdóttir 2012). In the peer-learning activities used for the three case studies, taking adequate time to describe one's own programme, the context for career services in the participating countries and the educational experience of participants was very fruitful for the continuation of joint work. The sharing of any written material in advance of the peer-learning event is also important and serves a similar purpose. Language issues are related but need additional consideration. Although the working language of the NICE network is English, not all members are equally confident and fluent English speakers. English language knowledge cannot be assumed and it is recommended that these issues be dealt with openly in the beginning of any collaboration. Amongst possible measures, interpreters can be organised as was done successfully in one of our peer-learning events.

The cooperative culture in the NICE network, as well as the local experiences and the CPRs, are the cornerstones of successful peer learning, firmly situated within policy frameworks and quality processes of European higher education. Together, the three resources of jointly constructed CPRs, local experiences and a cooperative culture of networking, provide a fertile ground to enhance the quality of academic training in career guidance and counselling. Constructive and well-conducted peer learning can play a key role in optimising the use of knowledge resources among the NICE members and can help to sustain the collaborative culture already created. Moreover, peer learning can be used to approach many facets of quality, including curriculum, teaching and approaches to stakeholder cooperation, as can be seen in the summary of examples of use of the CPRs among the NICE partners presented here and in Chapter 6. Hopefully, the guidelines for peer learning will support the future work for quality enhancement, community building and increased professionalization in career guidance and counselling.

Acknowledgements

The European Competence Standards (ECS), which lie at the heart of this publication, build on the achievements of prior work done in our field internationally, and in various countries at the national level. Our first proposal of NICE Core Competences (NICE 2012) already drew heavily on the competence frameworks of the IAEVG (2003) and Cedefop (2009), in addition to several national frameworks (see Katsarov et al. 2012). New inspiration has come from the DICBDPEC project (2013), a European reference profile for PES and EURES counsellors (PES to PES 2014) and the INNO-CAREER project (2014). Similarly, the NICE frameworks have been inspired by the developments concerning lifelong guidance policy in Europe. In particular, our work builds on the council resolutions on lifelong guidance (Council of the European Union 2004; 2008), the work of the OECD (2004; OECD & EU 2004), Cedefop (2005; 2008; 2009; 2011) and the European Lifelong Guidance Policy Network, particularly the European Resource Kit (ELGPN 2012). We would like to express our gratitude to all people and organisations, who have contributed to the discussion, which competences are needed in the field of career guidance and counselling. Without these prior achievements and simultaneous developments, the arriving at the ECS would have been impossible.

A special thank you in this sense goes to the European Commission, which hasn't only funded the project, which led to the development of the European Competence Standards. Indeed, the European Commission has played a central role over the past decades in creating awareness for questions of quality and professionalism in career guidance and counselling, and bringing relevant actors together.

Furthermore, we would like to express our sincere gratitude to all those who shared their comments and ideas with us during the European Summit for Developing the Career Workforce of the Future in Canterbury (September 3-4, 2014) and who participated in the public consultation on the first draft of the ECS from September to November 2014. More than 100 stakeholders from 33 European countries have supported us in refining the NICE Memorandum and the ECS over the past years. Your valuable comments, critiques and suggestions have been immensely helpful in preparing a framework, which we hope will be of use all across Europe in the future (Katsarov et al. 2015).

Finally, we, as the editors, would like to thank our dear colleagues from the NICE 2 project, for the great experience of working together in the past years. The following people have actively contributed to the concepts presented in this handbook, taking part in diverse workshops and projects concerned with peer learning, training innovation, and competence standards. Additionally, many of them have also played a significant role in managing our network strategically (the Steering Committee), promoting the exchange of staff and students in our network (the Mobility Team), sharing news within and outside the network (the Website & Newsletter Team), and working towards the quality and sustainability of the network (the Quality Group). We therefore thank all contributors to the NICE Memorandum and the European Competence Standards (in alphabetical order): Graham Allan, Salim Atay, Toni Babarovic, Mihaela Badea, Stella Blöndal, Randi Boelskifte Skovhus, Baiba Briede, Cristina Ceinos, Anne Chant, Banu Cirakoglu, Valérie Cohen-Scali, Ana Couce, Petya Dankova, Jean-Pierre Dauwalder, Nikos Drosos, Maria Eduarda Duarte, Sif Einarsdóttir, Bernd-Joachim Ertelt, Elena Fernández, Lea Ferrari, Zuzana Freibergová, Andreas Frey, Rebeca García, Laura Gressnerová, Erik Hagaseth Haug, Lucy Hearne, Lenka Hloušková, Johannes Katsarov, Jaana Kettunen, István Kiss, Andrej Kohont, Alain Kokosowski, Seija Koskela, Jolanta Kavale, Monika Kukyte, Christine Lagabrielle, Jukka Lerkkanen, Mia Lindberg, Anders Lovén, Ande Magus, Koorosh Massoudi, Dione Mifsud, Janet Moffett, Rachel Mulvey, Lijana Navickiene, Sasa Niklanovic, Miguel Nogueira, Helle Nordentoft, Laura Nota, Czesław Noworol, Hazel Reid, Janis Pavulens, Monika Petermandl, Roberta Piazza, Peter Plant, Jacques Pouyaud, Ivan Prelovský, Nathalie Prudhomme, Kestutis Pukelis, Sauli Puukari, Margit Rammo, Jérôme Rossier, Jean-Jacques Ruppert, Christiane Schiersmann, Nicolas Schöpf, Torild Schulstok, Teresa Sgaramella, Despoina Sidiropoulou-Dimakakou, Grzegorz Sikorski, Luis Sobrado, Inita Soika, Salvatore Soresi, Emil Stan, Tim Theeboom, Rie Thomsen, Štefan Vendel, Inge Van Der Putten, Annelies Van Vianen, Guðbjörg Vilhjálmsdóttir, Raimo Vuorinen, Peter C. Weber, Frida Wikstrand, Jan Woldendorp, Julia Yates, and Anda Zvigule. A list and map of all partner organisations can be found at the end of the handbook.

Last but not least, we would like to thank the people who have enabled this publication very much for the excellent cooperation: Miriam von Maydell from Barbara Budrich Publishers and Sonya Katsarova for the layout and design of the handbook.

Appendix

Appendix 1: The Bergen Communiqué (Bergen 2005)

Framework of Qualifications for the European Higher Education Area

The Bergen Conference of European Ministers Responsible for Higher Education 19-20 May 2005 adopted the overarching framework for qualifications in the EHEA, comprising three cycles (including, within national contexts, the possibility of intermediate qualifications), generic descriptors for each cycle based on learning outcomes and competences, and credit ranges in the first and second cycles. Ministers committed themselves to elaborating national frameworks for qualifications compatible with the overarching framework for qualifications in the EHEA by 2010, and to having started work on this by 2007.

	Outcomes	**ECTS Credits**
First cycle qualification	Qualifications that signify completion of the **first cycle** are awarded to students who: • have demonstrated knowledge and understanding in a field of study that builds upon their general secondary education, and is typically at a level that, whilst supported by advanced textbooks, includes some aspects that will be informed by knowledge of the forefront of their field of study; • can apply their knowledge and understanding in a manner that indicates a professional approach to their work or vocation, and have competences typically demonstrated through devising and sustaining arguments and solving problems within their field of study; • have the ability to gather and interpret relevant data (usually within their field of study) to inform judgments that include reflection on relevant social, scientific or ethical issues; • can communicate information, ideas, problems and solutions to both specialist and non-specialist audiences; • have developed those learning skills that are necessary for them to continue to undertake further study with a high degree of autonomy.	Typically include 180-240 ECTS credits

Second cycle qualification	Qualifications that signify completion of the **second cycle** are awarded to students who: • have demonstrated knowledge and understanding that is founded upon and extends and/or enhances that typically associated with the first cycle, and that provides a basis or opportunity for originality in developing and/or applying ideas, often within a research context; • can apply their knowledge and understanding, and problem solving abilities in new or unfamiliar environments within broader (or multidisciplinary) contexts related to their field of study; • have the ability to integrate knowledge and handle complexity, and formulate judgments with incomplete or limited information, but that include reflecting on social and ethical responsibilities linked to the application of their knowledge and judgments; • can communicate their conclusions, and the knowledge and rationale underpinning these, to specialist and non-specialist audiences clearly and unambiguously; • have the learning skills to allow them to continue to study in a manner that may be largely self-directed or autonomous.	Typically include 90-120 ECTS credits, with a minimum of 60 credits at the level of the 2nd cycle
Third cycle qualification	Qualifications that signify completion of the **third cycle** are awarded to students who: • have demonstrated a systematic understanding of a field of study and mastery of the skills and methods of research associated with that field; • have demonstrated the ability to conceive, design, implement and adapt a substantial process of research with scholarly integrity; • have made a contribution through original research that extends the frontier of knowledge by developing a substantial body of work, some of which merits national or international refereed publication; • are capable of critical analysis, evaluation and synthesis of new and complex ideas; • can communicate with their peers, the larger scholarly community and the society in general about their areas of expertise; • can be expected to be able to promote, within academic and professional contexts, technological, social or cultural advancement in a knowledge based society.	Not specified

Appendix 2: Resources to Support Quality Assurance

Standards and Guidelines for Quality Assurance in the European Higher Education Area (ESG 2015)

Common standards and guidelines prepared by EUA, ENQA, EURASHE, the European Students Union, Education International, Business Europe, and EQAR. Approved by the Ministerial Conference in May 2015 in Yerevan.

Link: http://www.enqa.eu/index.php/home/esg/ (already available in 10 languages)

Bologna Process – European Higher Education Area

The official website on the Bologna Process, which provides access to all of the relevant policy documents and information on events and other available materials.

Link: http://www.ehea.info/

ECTS User's Guide (2015)

The European Credit Transfer and Accumulation System (ECTS) is a tool of the European Higher Education Area for making studies and courses more transparent and thus helping to enhance the quality of higher education.

Link: http://ec.europa.eu/education/library/publications/2015/ects-users-guide_en.pdf

European Association for Quality Assurance in Higher Education (ENQA)

ENQA promotes European co-operation in the field of quality assurance in higher education and disseminates information and expertise among its members and towards stakeholders in order to develop and share good practice and to foster the European dimension of quality assurance.

Link: http://www.enqa.eu/

European Quality Assurance Register for Higher Education (EQAR)

EQAR is a register of quality assurance agencies that demonstrate compliance with the European Standards and Guidelines for Quality Assurance (ESG 2015) through an external review by independent experts.

Link: https://www.eqar.eu/

European University Association (EUA)

With respect to quality assurance, EUA seeks to ensure that the views of the university sector are taken into account in European and national-level policy discussions on internal and external quality assurance.

Link: http://www.eua.be/policy-representation/quality-assurance.aspx

References

Bergen Communiqué (2005). *The framework of qualifications for the European Higher Education Area.* Bergen Conference of European Ministers Responsible for Higher Education 19-20 May 2005. Available at www.ehea.info/Uploads/Declarations/Bergen_Communique1.pdf.

Bergsmann, E., M.-T. Schultes, P. Winter, B. Schober & C. Spiel (2015). Evaluation of competence-based teaching in higher education: From theory to practice. *Evaluation and Program Planning*, Vol. 52, pp. 1-9.

Berlin Communiqué (2003). *Realising the European Higher Education Area*, Communiqué of the Conference of Ministers responsible for Higher Education in Berlin on 19 September 2003. Available at www.ehea.info/Uploads/Declarations/Berlin_Communique1.pdf.

Bloom, B., M. Engelhart, E. Furst, W. Hill & D. Krathwohl (1956). *Taxonomy of Educational Objectives. Volume I: The Cognitive Domain.* New York: McKay.

Bloom, B., B. Masia & D. Krathwohl (1964). *Taxonomy of Educational Objectives. Volume II: The Affective Domain.* New York: McKay.

Bologna Declaration (1999). *Joint declaration of the European Ministers of Education of 19 June 1999.* Available at www.ehea.info/Uploads/Declarations/BOLOGNA_DECLARATION1.pdf.

Borders, L. D. (1991). A Systematic Approach to Peer Group Supervision. *Journal of Counseling & Development.* Vol 69, 1/1991, pp. 248-252.

Bucharest Communiqué (2012). *Making the Most of Our Potential: Consolidating the European Higher Education Area*, Communiqué of the Conference of Ministers responsible for Higher Education in Bucharest on 26-27 April 2012. Available at http://bologna-bucharest2012.ehea.info/background-documents.html.

CEDEFOP (2005). *Improving Lifelong Guidance Policies and Systems – Using Common Reference Tools*, edited by J. Wannan and J. McCarthy. Luxembourg: European Centre for the Development of Vocational Training (CEDEFOP).

CEDEFOP (2008). *From Policy to Practice. A Systemic Change to Lifelong Guidance in Europe*, edited by R. Sultana. Luxembourg: European Centre for the Development of Vocational Training (CEDEFOP).

CEDEFOP (2009). *Professionalizing Career Guidance. Practitioner Competences and Qualification Routes in Europe*, edited by L. Barham. Luxembourg: European Centre for the Development of Vocational Training (CEDEFOP).

CEDEFOP (2011). *Lifelong Guidance across Europe: Reviewing Policy Progress and Future Prospects*, edited by M. Launikari. Luxembourg: European Centre for the Development of Vocational Training (CEDEFOP).

Cohen, L., L. Manion & K. Morrison (2011). *Research Methods in Education*, 7th Edition: Oxon, Abingdon: Routledge.

Council of the European Union (2004). *Resolution on Strengthening Policies, Systems and Practices in the Field of Guidance throughout the Life in Europe*. Resolution No. 8448/04 EDUC 89 SOC 179: Brussels, 18 May. Available at data.consilium.europa.eu/doc/document/ST-8448-2004-INIT/en/pdf.

Council of the European Union (2008). Resolution on Better Integrating Lifelong Guidance into Lifelong Learning Strategies. Resolution No. 14398/08 EDUC 241 SOC 607: Brussels, 31 October. Available at data.consilium.europa.eu/doc/document/ST-14398-2008-INIT/en/pdf.

DICBDPEC (2013a). *Career Guidance and Human Resource Management. Bachelor's study programme*, edited by L. Gressnerová & I. Prelovský. Bratislava: Slovak University of Technology in Bratislava. Available at www.ies.stuba.sk/erasmus/file.php/1/BA_study_programme.pdf.

DICBDPEC (2013b). *Career Guidance in Education, Profession and Labour Market Management. Master's study programme*, edited by L. Gressnerová & I. Prelovský. Bratislava: Slovak University of Technology in Bratislava.

Dahrendorf, R. (1958). Homo Sociologicus. Versuch zur Geschichte, Bedeutung und Kritik der Kategorie der sozialen Rolle, in: R. Dahrendorf: *Pfade aus Utopia*. Munich: Piper, pp. 128-194.

ECTS Users' Guide (2015). Luxembourg: Publications Office of the European Union. Available at http://ec.europa.eu/education/library/publications/2015/ects-users-guide_en.pdf.

Einarsdóttir, S. (2012). Competences of higher education faculty members. In NICE: *NICE Handbook for the Academic Training of Career Guidance and Counselling Professionals*. Heidelberg: Heidelberg University, pp. 129–134.

ELGPN (2012). *Lifelong Guidance Policy Development: A European Resource Kit*, edited by R. Vuorinen and A. Watts. Jyväskylä: European Lifelong Guidance Policy Network.

ENQA (2009). *Report on Standards and Guidelines for Quality Assurance in the European Higher Education Area*. Helsinki: European Association for Quality Assurance in Higher Education. Available at ecahe.eu/w/images/3/3c/Standards_and_Guidelines_for_Quality_Assurance_in_the_European_Higher_Education_Area.pdf.

EQF (2008). The European Qualifications Framework for Lifelong Learning. Luxembourg: Publications Office of the European Union. Available at https://ec.europa.eu/ploteus/sites/eac-eqf/files/broch_en.pdf.

Ertelt, B.-J., P. Weber & J. Katsarov (2012). Existing Degree Programmes in Europe, in NICE: *NICE Handbook for the Academic Training of Career Guidance and Counselling Professionals*. Heidelberg: Heidelberg University, pp. 83-104.

ESG (2015). *Standards and Guidelines for Quality Assurance in the European Higher Education Area*, prepared by EUA, ENQA, EURASHE, ESU, Education International, Business Europe and EQAR, approved by the Ministerial Conference in Yerevan, 14-15 May 2015. Available at http://www.enqa.eu/index.php/home/esg/.

European Commission (2014). *Progress in Quality Assurance in Higher Education*. COM (2014) 29. Luxembourg: Publications Office of the European Union. Available at ecahe.eu/assets/uploads/2014/01/EU-Report-on-Progress-in-Quality-Assurance-in-Higher-Education-2014.pdf.

European Commission, EACEA & Eurydice (2015). *The European Higher Education Area in 2015: Bologna Process Implementation Report*. Luxembourg: Publications Office of the European Union. Available at www.ehea.info/Uploads/SubmitedFiles/5_2015/132824.pdf.

Evetts, J. (2011). Professionalism in Turbulent Times: Challenges to and Opportunities for Professionalism as an Occupational Value, *Journal of the National Institute for Career Education and Counselling* (NICEC), Nov. 2011, Issue 27, pp. 8-16.

Hearne, L. (2011). The Consideration of a Constructivist Evaluation Framework in Adult Guidance Practice, *Australian Journal of Career Development*, 30, (3), pp. 31-38.

IAEVG (2003). International Competencies for Educational and Vocational Guidance Practitioners. Bern: International Association for Educational and Vocational Guidance. Available at iaevg.net/wp-content/uploads/Competencies-English1.pdf.

INNO-CAREER (2014). *Common Occupational Profile & Standards*. INNO-CAREER Erasmus Project. Athens: National Organisation for the Certification of Qualifications and Vocational Guidance EOPPEP. Available at www.inno-career.eu/docs/deliverables/3.2.%20COMMON%20OCCUPATIONAL%20PROFILE%20AND%20STANDARDS.pdf.

Kant, I. (1993) [1785]. Grounding for the Metaphysics of Morals, with: On a supposed right to lie because of philanthropic concerns. 3th Edition. Indianapolis: Hackett.

Katsarov, J., E. Dörr & P. Weber (2012): The NICE Core Competences in Comparison with other National and International Competence Frameworks, in NICE: *NICE Handbook for the Academic Training of Career Guidance and Counselling Professionals.* Heidelberg: Heidelberg University, pp. 231-238.

Katsarov, J., J. Lerkkanen, J. Pouyaud & K. Pukelis (2015): European Competence Standards – Feedback, Insights and Changes, in: *NICE Newsletter* 1/2015, p. 2-5. Available at http://journals.ub.uni-heidelberg.de/index.php/nice/issue/view/2144.

Krathwohl D., B. Bloom & B. Masia (1964). *Taxonomy of Educational Objectives Volume II: The Affective Domain.* New York: McKay.

Le Boterf, G. (2014). *Construire les Compétences Individuelles et Collectives.* 6th Edition. Paris: Eyrolles.

Leuven & Louvain-la-Neuve Communiqué (2009). The Bologna 2020 Process. European Ministers Responsible for Higher Education. Available at www.ehea.info/Uploads/Declarations/Leuven_Louvain-la-Neuve_Communiqu%C3%A9_April_2009.pdf.

Maastricht Treaty (1992). *Treaty on European Union.* Council of the European Communities & Commission of the European Communities. Luxembourg: Publications Office of the European Union.

McLeod, J. (2015). *Doing Research in Counselling and Psychotherapy*, 3rd Edition. London: Sage.

Moon, J. (2002). *How to use level descriptors.* London: University of East London.

Mulder, M., J. Gulikers, H. Biemans & R. Wesselink (2009). The new competence concept in higher education: error or enrichment? *Journal of European Industrial Training*, Vol. 33, pp. 755-770.

NICE (2012). *NICE Handbook for the Academic Training of Career Guidance and Counselling Professionals*, edited by C. Schiersmann, B. Ertelt, J. Katsarov, R. Mulvey, H. Reid & P. Weber. Heidelberg: Heidelberg University. [References refer to the English full version of the handbook, i.e. not to the short version called Common Points of Reference] Available at www.nice-network.eu/wp-content/uploads/2015/11/NICE_Handbook_full_version_online.pdf.

OECD (2003). *The Definition and Selection of Key Competencies. Executive Summary.* Paris: Organisation for Economic Co-operation and Development (OECD). Available at www.oecd.org/pisa/35070367.pdf

OECD (2004). *Career Guidance and Public Policy – Bridging the Gap*, edited by R. Sweet & A. Watts. Paris: Organisation for Economic Co-operation and Development (OECD).

OECD & EU (2004). *Career Guidance. A Handbook for Policy Makers*, edited by R. Sultana and A. Watts. Paris/Luxembourg: Organisation for Economic Co-operation and Development (OECD) & European Communities.

PES to PES (2014). *European Reference Competence Profile for PES and EURES Counsellors.* Analytical paper produced by L. Sienkiewicz and R. Vuorinen as an outcome of the PES to PES Dialogue. Brussels: DG Employment, Social Affairs and Inclusion. Available at iccdpp.org/wp-content/uploads/2015/01/Analytical-paper-European-reference-competence-profile-for-PES-and-EURES-counsellors-2014-6.pdf.

Petermandl, M. (2014). Quality and sustainability of the NICE network. *NICE Newsletter* 2/2014. Available at http://journals.ub.uni-heidelberg.de/index.php/nice/issue/view/1439.

Petermandl, M., S. Einarsdóttir, J. Lerkkanen & P. Weber (2014). Results of the 2nd Quality Survey. Presented at the NICE Conference in Canterbury, Sept. 6, 2014.

Pukelis, K. (2011). Study Programme Designing and Renewal: Learning Outcomes Paradigm, *The Quality of Higher Education (Aukštojo mokslo kokybė)* 08/2011, pp. 38-73.

Reid, H. & B. Bassot (2012). Reflexivity. In NICE: *NICE Handbook for the Academic Training of Career Guidance and Counselling Professionals.* Heidelberg: Heidelberg University, pp. 179-183.

Romsek, B. S., K. LeRoux & J. M. Blackmar (2012). A preliminary theory of informal accountability among network organizational actors. *Public Administration Review*, 72(39), pp. 442-453.

Scharmer, C. O. (2007). *Theory U: Leading from the Future as it Emerges.* Cambridge: The Society for Organizational Learning.

Schiersmann, C. & H.-U. Thiel (2014). *Organisationsentwicklung. Prinzipien und Strategien von Veränderungsprosessen*, 4th Edition. Wiesbaden: Springer VS.

Schiersmann, C. & P. Weber (2013). Gesamtkonzept für Qualität von Beratung, in: *Beratung in Bildung, Beruf und Beschäftigung. Eckpunkte und Erprobung eines integrierten Qualitätskonzepts*, edited by C. Schiersmann & P. Weber. Bielefeld: WBV, pp. 41-54.

Schimank, U. (2011). *Handeln und Strukturen. Einführung in die akteurstheoretische Soziologie.* 3th Edition. Weinheim: Juventa.

Sorbonne Declaration (1998). *Joint declaration on harmonisation of the architecture of the European hig-

her education system by the four Ministers in charge for France, Germany, Italy and the United Kingdom, Paris, the Sorbonne, May 25 1998. Available at www.ehea.info/Uploads/Declarations/SORBONNE_DECLARATION1.pdf.

Sultana, R. (2009). Competence and competence frameworks in career guidance: complex and contested concepts, *International Journal for Educational and Vocational Guidance*, 9, pp. 15-30.

Tietse, K.-O. (2013). *Kollegiale Beratung. Problemlösungen gemeinsam entwickeln*. 6th Edition. Reinbek: Rowohlt Taschenbuch Verlag.

Topping, K. J. (2001). Peer assisted learning: A framework for consultation. *Journal of Educational and Psychological Consultation*, 12(2), pp. 113-132.

Topping, K. J. (2005). Trends in Peer Learning, *Educational Psychology*, 25 (6), pp. 631-645.

Tuning (2008). *Tuning Educational Structures in Europe. Universities' contribution to the Bologna Process. An Introduction*, 2nd Edition, Bilbao: University of Deusto.

Watts, A. & R. van Esbroeck (1998). *News Skills for New Futures. Higher Education Guidance and Counselling Services in the European Union*. VUB Press / FEDORA: Brussels / Louvain-la-Neuve.

Weber, P. (2013). *Qualität in der arbeitsweltlichen Beratung. Eine Untersuchung von Qualitätsmerkmalen, Qualitätsmodellen und eines Netzwerks zu deren politischen Implementierung in Europa unter Berücksichtigung der Theorie der Selbstorganisation*. Dissertation. Heidelberg: Heidelberg University.

Weber, P. & J. Katsarov (2013). Die "Offene Methode der Koordinierung" als Ansatz zur Verbesserung der Qualität in der Beratung in Bildung, Beruf und Beschäftigung, in: *Beratung in Bildung, Beruf und Beschäftigung. Eckpunkte und Erprobung eines integrierten Qualitätskonzepts*, edited by C. Schiersmann & P. Weber. Bielefeld: WBV, pp. 55-94.

Weber, P. (2015). Pedagogy and Organizational Learning – Theoretical Reflections on Synergetics as a Meta-Model for Designing and Researching Learning Processes in Organizations. In: Gröhlich et al.: *Tagungsband. Organisationspädagogik und Theorie. Beiträge der AG Organisationspädagogik*. Heidelberg: Springer VS.

Yin, R.K. (2009). *Case Study Research: Design and Methods*. 4th edition. Thousand Oaks: Sage.

The NICE Glossary

The following glossary comprises terms used in this NICE Handbook in a standardised way. Many of the terms reflect the common language, which we have tried to develop in NICE through our collaboration on identifying common points of reference (CPR). Some of the terms, which were defined in the first NICE Handbook (NICE 2012), have been replaced or refined. This refers, in particular, to the titles of the NICE Professional Roles and the modules of the NICE Curriculum Framework.

The glossary is a common achievement of NICE and draws on the work and contributions of many colleagues. In its current version, it has been prepared by the editors of the handbook.

Academic cycles	The Bologna Process harmonised three academic cycles across Europe. Bachelor's, Master's and PhD level degree programmes sit at the EQF levels 6, 7 and 8 respectively.
Academic training	In NICE, we prefer to speak of academic training, when we refer to higher education offers in career guidance and counselling. The term 'training' stresses the practice-orientation of such offers. The term 'academic' emphasises that career practitioners should engage in specialised offers of higher education as an entry requirement for their practice.
Affective resources	Psychosocial resources that bring about the motivation and volition (individual will) of people to do the right thing. Important types of affective resources are internalised values and attitudes. In the NICE Curriculum Framework, affective resources are a type of learning outcome. The EQF does not spell out generic level descriptors for learning outcomes in terms of affective resources. Instead, the area of "responsibility" is included in the level descriptors for the domain of competence.
Attitudes	A type of learning outcome and a type of psychosocial resource, upon which competence is based. In the NICE Curriculum Framework, attitudes are featured in the category of affective resources. The EQF doesn't spell out generic level descriptors for learning outcomes in terms of values and attitudes. Instead, the area of "responsibility" is included in the level descriptors for the domain of competence.
BA	Bachelor, see academic cycles.
Behavioural resources	Behavioural resources are frequently referred to as skills or know-how. They are action-oriented psychosocial resources and are based on practice in doing something. Cognitive skills include logical, intuitive and creative thinking as well as the application of knowledge. Practical skills involve manual dexterity, the use of methods, materials, tools and instruments. In the NICE Curriculum Framework, behavioural resources are a type of learning outcome. They correspond with the domain of skills in the EQF.
Career Advisor	One of the NTCPs: Career Advisors are important sources of basic information and support for people facing career-related challenges. Career Advisors are teachers, placement managers, psychologists, social workers or public administrators (among others). They are not career professionals, but professionals in another field, who offer some career support in addition to their primary roles and tasks. Often they are the first persons to whom people come for advice. They should be able to offer basic support and advice at a reliable level of quality and immediately understand when a person would benefit from professional career services, which is why we also define competence standards for them.

Career Assessment & Information	One of the NPRs: Career Assessment & Information describes the professional role of career practitioners to support people in attaining relevant information about themselves (e.g. their interests, talents and competences), the labour market, and educational or vocational options – depending on their individual information needs. In NICE 2012, we referred to "Career Information & Assessment". We have changed the order because there should first be an assessment of the informational needs of clients, before they receive relevant information.
Career Counselling	One of the NPRs: Career Counselling describes the professional role of career practitioners to support people in making sense of the situations they are experiencing, working through issues towards solutions, making difficult career decisions, and realising personal change.
Career Education	One of the NPRs: Career Education describes the professional role of career practitioners to support people in developing their career management competences, i.e. the competences, which they need for career-related learning and development.
Career guidance and counselling (CGC)	In NICE we have agreed to generally refer to "career guidance and counselling" (CGC) as a fixed term for the description of our field of research and academic training. The NICE Professional Roles, which we identify as central to the practice of career guidance and counselling, comprise career counselling, career education, career assessment and information, social systems interventions and career service management. See Chapter 4 in NICE 2012 for more information.
Career management competences	The competences, which people need in order to shape their educational paths and their work lives autonomously and responsibly. Career management competences include the ability to become aware of own resources and needs, understanding the functioning of labour markets, vocational and educational systems, the mature use of career information systems, developing career plans, making career decisions, adapting to change pro-actively, self-presentation skills etc.
Career Practitioner	When we speak of career practitioners, we mean all people involved in the provision of career guidance and counselling, whether they do so as full Career Professionals, in addition to their primary occupation in another field (as Career Advisors), or in some kind of special function (as Career Specialists). We therefore distinguish three types of career practitioners, the NICE Types of Career Practitioners (NCTPs).

Career Professional	One of the NTCPs: Career Professionals are dedicated to CGC and see it as their vocation to support people in dealing with complex career-related challenges. In addition to the basic support offered by Career Advisors, Career Professionals need to be ready to support people who are facing uncertainty, multi-faceted problems and unpredictable situations, knowing that their career decisions could have a heavy impact on their lives. They support the development of strategic approaches, offer access to highly specialised knowledge, and help clients in facing stressful phases of transition and projects of personal change.
Career Specialist	One of the NTCPs: Career Specialists take on a special responsibility for the career profession and work towards the advancement of career guidance and counselling (CGC) in different ways. Some of them concentrate on practical matters, e.g. the management of career services, policy-making or the supervision of career practitioners. Others primarily engage in research and development or academic training in CGC. In addition to their ability to practise as Career Professionals, Career Specialists need to demonstrate substantial authority, scholarly and professional integrity in a particular area of CGC.
Career service	Career services refer to the provision of career guidance and counselling through different types of career practitioners.
Career Service Management	One of the NPRs: Career Service Management describes the professional role of career practitioners to manage themselves and assure the quality of their work.
CEDEFOP	European Centre for the Development of Vocational Training
CGC	Career Guidance and Counselling
Cognitive resources	Psychosocial resources, which mainly reflect knowledge that people have and can use to find solutions to specific questions or problems. Cognitive resources go beyond information (who, what, when) and comprise the understanding of theories (why, how). In the NICE Curriculum Framework, cognitive resources are a type of learning outcome. They correspond with the domain of knowledge in the EQF.
Common points of reference (CPR)	In higher education, CPR provide a common language and understanding of central phenomena of the particular area of academic training. CPR provide orientation for higher education institutions, while not inhibiting their freedom to provide the individual, tailor-made study programmes, which best fit the needs of their relevant stakeholders. In NICE, we have developed the following CPR: the NICE Professional Roles (2015; 2012), the NICE Core Competences (2012), the NICE Curriculum Framework (2012), the NICE Glossary (2015; 2012) and the European Competence Standards (2015).

Competence	The ability of people to meet complex demands in particular situations, drawing upon adequate psychosocial resources in a reflective manner. When we speak of competences in this handbook, we are talking about a specific educative concept, which builds a link between the more detailed types of learning outcomes for academic training and the requirements of the labour market. The EQF defines generic level descriptors for the domain of competences in terms of autonomy and responsibility.
Competence-based learning	The aim of competence-based learning is to enable students to develop the competences, which they need to address the real-life challenges, which they will need to be able to deal with in practice.
Competence standard	A shared agreement about the minimum level of competence needed to perform a particular task. Competence standards define a common threshold in terms of the competences required for a particular practice: competences, which should be measurable in terms of a predefined quality-level of practice through level descriptors.
Core competence	The concept of core competences as in the NICE Core Competences (2012) has been replaced by the concept of competence standards with this second volume of the NICE Handbook.
ECS	European Competence Standards for the Academic Training of Career Practitioners, see: European Competence Standards
ECTS	Degree programmes in Europe award credit points to students based on the European Credit Transfer and Accumulation System (ECTS) to increase transparency and comparability between degrees in European member states. The use of this credit accumulation and transfer system also encourages the modularisation of degree programmes and generally aims at enabling more flexibility in higher education (e.g. in terms of learning mobility).
EHEA	European Higher Education Area
ENQA	European Association for Quality Assurance in Higher Education
EQAR	European Quality Assurance Register for Higher Education
EQF	European Qualification Framework for Lifelong Learning (2008)
ELGPN	European Lifelong Guidance Policy Network
EU	European Union
European Competence Standards (ECS)	The competence standards for the academic training of career practitioners, which NICE has first published in 2015.
HEI	Higher Education Institution
HR	Human Resources
IAEVG	International Association for Educational and Vocational Guidance
ICT	Information and Communication Technology

Generic professional competences	The generic professional competences hold the other competences together as meta-competences and are relevant for the practice of all professional roles. They are based on the generic professional tasks, which have been identified as part of the task profiles of the three NICE Types of Career Practitioners.
Generic professional tasks	Some of the tasks, which we identified as part of the task profiles of the three NICE Types of Career Practitioners, are relevant for several professional roles. This is why we define them in an additional category called generic professional tasks. This means that they are important for all of the professional roles.
Knowledge	A type of learning outcome and a type of psychosocial resource, upon which competence is based. In the NICE Curriculum Framework, knowledge is featured in the category of cognitive resources. Cognitive resources go beyond information (who, what, when) and comprise the understanding of theories (why, how). The EQF defines generic level descriptors for learning outcomes in the domain of knowledge.
Learning outcomes	Learning outcomes are statements of what learners know, understand, and are able to do upon completion of a particular learning process. Through the description of learning outcomes, degree programmes and qualifications are supposed to become understandable and comparable. In the NICE Curriculum Framework (2012), learning outcomes for the academic training of career practitioners are determined in terms of competences and in terms of relevant resource requirements.
Level descriptors	The definition of measurable competences and competence standards requires the definition of a quality level at which a particular activity must be performed. Level descriptors are defined by expressing the context/ circumstances under which an activity shall be performed and/or which measurable outcomes are expected. The EQF (2008) offers generic level descriptors for eight qualification levels for the domains of knowledge, skills and competence.
Lifelong guidance	The provision of career services to all members of society at all stages of their careers.
Lifelong learning	The continuous education of all people in terms of citizenship and employability.
MA	Master, see: academic cycles.
NCTPs	See: NICE Types of Career Practitioners
NICE	Network for Innovation in Career Guidance and Counselling in Europe
NICE Core Competences	The concept of core competences as in the NICE Core Competences (2012) has been replaced by the concept of European Competence Standards (ECS) with the second volume of the NICE Handbook (2015).

NICE Curriculum	In the NICE Curriculum (2012), learning outcomes in terms of competences and resource requirements are combined with suggestions for teaching, learning and assessment methods in nine modules.
NICE Professional Roles (NPRs)	The NPRs together represent what we consider to be the professional roles of career practitioners across Europe. To live up to their societal mission, all career practitioners should be able to perform in each of the NPRs to a greater or lesser extent, and consider all of them as part of their professional identity. The minimum extent, to which the NPRs should be integrated in the practice of the NICE Types of Career Practitioners, is defined in their task profiles.
NICE Types of Career Practitioners (NTCPs)	We distinguish between three types of career practitioners: Career Advisors, Career Professionals and Career Specialists. Each of these types of career practitioners has a distinct task profile. Competence standards are defined for each type.
NPRs	See: NICE Professional Roles
Peer learning	Peer learning generally refers to group strategies that involve learning through other learners (Topping 2001). In the context of academic training in career guidance and counselling, peer learning refers to planned workshops or meetings with the purpose of improving a study programme in a collegial way.
PES	Public Employment Service
Professional roles	Professional Roles define the broader societal expectations associated with a particular profession. They provide professionals and their clients with a basic idea about the profession.
Psychosocial resources	Affective, behavioural, and cognitive resources are considered to be relevant categories of psychosocial resources for competence. In the NICE Curriculum Framework, learning outcomes are defined for these three types of resources.
QAA	See: Quality Assurance Agency
QAE	Quality Assurance and Enhancement summarizes all formal and informal activities of higher education institutions to assure and enhance the quality of their study programmes. See: Quality assurance and quality enhancement.
Quality assurance	Quality assurance relates to the activities undertaken by universities and programme leaders to ensure the quality of a degree programme from the outset.
Quality Assurance Agency (QAA)	QAAs assess quality standards, evaluate institutions, accredit degree programmes or benchmark the performance of higher education institutions against each other (most of them at the national level).

Quality enhancement	Quality enhancement relates to diverse activities to improve the quality of a degree programme continuously once the programme is delivered.
Skills	A type of learning outcome and a type of psychosocial resource, upon which competence is based. In the NICE Curriculum Framework, skills are featured in the category of behavioural resources. Cognitive skills include logical, intuitive and creative thinking as well as the application of knowlege. Practical skills involve manual dexterity, the use of methods, materials, tools and instruments. The EQF defines generic level descriptors for learning outcomes in the domain of skills.
Social Systems Interventions	One of the NPRs: Social Systems Interventions describes the professional role of career practitioners to support people and organisations in designing and developing adequate career pathways.
Task	Tasks explain to the public what career practitioners actually do in practice. The purpose of task descriptions is to offer a clear idea about a person's job, which is also understandable for laypersons.
Task profile	Task profiles, which comprise several tasks, are used in human resource management to define the occupation of an employee or a category of employees.
Values	A type of learning outcome and a type of psychosocial resource, upon which competence is based. In the NICE Curriculum Framework, values are featured in the category of affective resources. The EQF does not spell out generic level descriptors for learning outcomes in terms of values and attitudes. Instead, the area of "responsibility" is included in the level descriptors for the domain of competence.

Partners of NICE from 2012 to 2015

Map of Europe: © Depositphotos

- Danube University Krems (Austria)
- University of Economics Varna (Bulgaria)
- Czech National Training Fund (Czech Republic)
- Masaryk University Brno (Czech Republic)
- University of Nicosia (Cyprus)
- Aarhus University (Denmark)
- INNOVE Foundation for Lifelong Learning Development (Estonia)
- European Society for Vocational Designing and Counselling
- University of Jyväskylä (Finland)
- JAMK University of Applied Sciences (Finland)
- Conservatoire National des Arts et Métiers (France)
- University of Bordeaux (France)
- CREDIJ Association Paris (France)
- HdBA University of Applied Labour Studies (Germany)
- Heidelberg University (Germany)
- Johannes Katsarov | Research - Training - Network Coordination (Germany)
- University of Athens (Greece)
- Eötvös Loránd University Budapest (Hungary)
- University of Iceland (Iceland)
- University of Limerick (Ireland)
- University of Catania (Italy)
- University of Padua (Italy)
- Latvia University of Agriculture (Latvia)
- Vytautas Magnus University (Lithuania)
- AVOPP Applied Vocational Psychology and Policy Research Unit (Luxembourg)
- University of Malta (Malta)
- University of Amsterdam (Netherlands)
- Fontys University of Applied Science (Netherlands)
- Saxion University of Applied Science (Netherlands)
- Lillehammer University College (Norway)
- Jagiellonian University in Kraków (Poland)
- Jan Długosz University Czestochowa (Poland)
- University of Wrocław (Poland)
- University of Lisbon (Portugal)
- Petroleum-Gas University of Ploiesti (Romania)
- Slovak University of Technology in Bratislava (Slovakia)
- University of Presov (Slovakia)
- Career Consulting, Sasa Niklanovič (Slovenia)
- University of Santiago de Compostela (Spain)
- Malmö University (Sweden)
- University of Lausanne (Switzerland)
- Istanbul Technical University (Turkey)
- Marmara University Istanbul (Turkey)
- Canterbury Christ Church University (United Kingdom)
- University of East London (United Kingdom)
- University of West Scotland (United Kingdom)

IJREE – International Journal for Research on Extended Education

ISSN: 2196-3673
ISSN Online: 2196-7423
Volume 4, 2016
Published twice a year
Pages: Approx. 120
(Format B5–17x24)
Language: English

The International Journal for Research on Extended Education aims at creating international visibility and a stronger scientific profile for the research field of extended education. The Journal is published by a group of internationally renowned educational researchers and is funded by the German Research Foundation (DFG).

From early childhood to late adolescence, young people are enrolled in various public or private forms of educational arrangements. Some of them, particularly pre-school-aged children, attend kindergarten or participate in early learning courses. School-aged children often participate in school- or community-based programmes, forms of private tutoring or after-school activities such as art courses or academic clubs, or they attend all-day schools.

Find our journals on www.budrich-journals.com